The Complete Guide to the Great Pyrenees

Erin Hotovy

LP Media Inc. Publishing

Text copyright © 2019 by LP Media Inc.

All rights reserved.

No part of this book may be reproduced or transmitted in any form or by any means, electronic or mechanical, including photocopying, recording, or by an information storage and retrieval system - except by a reviewer who may quote brief passages in a review to be printed in a magazine or newspaper - without permission in writing from the publisher. For information address LP Media Inc. Publishing, 3178 253rd Ave. NW, Isanti, MN 55040

www.lpmedia.org

Publication Data

Erin Hotovy

The Complete Guide to the Great Pyrenees ---- First edition.

Summary: "Successfully raising a Great Pyrenees dog from puppy to old age" --- Provided by publisher.

ISBN: 978-1-69686-5-029

[1. Great Pyrenees --- Non-Fiction] I. Title.

This book has been written with the published intent to provide accurate and authoritative information in regard to the subject matter included. While every reasonable precaution has been taken in preparation of this book the author and publisher expressly disclaim responsibility for any errors, omissions, or adverse effects arising from the use or application of the information contained inside. The techniques and suggestions are to be used at the reader's discretion and are not to be considered a substitute for professional veterinary care. If you suspect a medical problem with your dog, consult your veterinarian.

Design by Sorin Rădulescu

First paperback edition, 2019

TABLE OF CONTENTS

CHAPTER 1
Great Pyrenees History 8
What Is a Great Pyrenees? 8
History of the Great Pyrenees 9
Physical Characteristics 10
Breed Behavioral Characteristics 11
Is a Great Pyrenees the Right Fit for You? 14

CHAPTER 2
Choosing a Great Pyrenees 16
Buying vs. Adopting 17
How to Find a Reputable Breeder 19
Researching Breeders 21
Health Tests and Certifications 22
Breeder Contracts and Guarantees 23
Choosing the Perfect Pup 24

CHAPTER 3
Preparing Your Home for Your Great Pyrenees 28
Adjusting Your Current Pets and Children 29
Dangerous Things that Dogs Might Eat 31
Other Household Dangers 33
Preparing Indoor Spaces 35
Preparing Outdoor Spaces 36

CHAPTER 4
Bringing Your Great Pyrenees Home — 38
The Importance of Having a Plan — 39
The Ride Home — 39
The First Night Home — 40
What to Expect in the First Few Weeks — 42
The First Vet Visit — 43
Puppy Classes — 44
Pet Supplies to Have Ready — 44
How Much Will This Cost? — 46

CHAPTER 5
Being a Puppy Parent — 48
Standing by Your Expectations — 49
How to Crate Train — 50
Chewing — 50
Barking — 53
Digging — 53
Separation Anxiety — 54
Running Away — 55
Bedtime — 56
Leaving Your Dog Home Alone — 56

CHAPTER 6
Housetraining — 58
Different Options for Housetraining — 58
Getting into a Routine — 59
Rewarding Positive Behavior — 60
Crate Training for Housetraining Use — 61
Playpens and Doggy Doors — 63

CHAPTER 7
Socializing with People and Animals — 64
Importance of Good Socialization — 65
Behavior Around Other Dogs — 66
Properly Greeting New People — 68
Great Pyrenees and Children — 69

CHAPTER 8
Great Pyrenees and Your Other Pets — 70
Introducing Your New Puppy to Other Pets — 71
Pack Mentality — 73
Fighting and Bad Behavior — 75
Raising Littermates — 76
What if My Pets Don't Get Along? — 77

CHAPTER 9
Physical and Mental Exercise — 78
Exercise Requirements — 79
Different Types of Exercise to Try — 81
Mental Exercise — 83

CHAPTER 10
Training Your Great Pyrenees — 86
Clear Expectations — 87
Operant Conditioning Basics — 88
Primary Reinforcements — 89
Secondary Reinforcements — 91
Dangers of Punishment — 92
Hiring a Trainer and Attending Classes — 95
Owner Behavior — 97

CHAPTER 11
Basic Commands — 98
Benefits of Proper Training — 98
Places to Practice — 99
Basic Commands — 100
- Sit — 100
- Stay — 101
- Down — 101
- Come — 102
- Drop It — 104
- Walk — 104
- Watch Me — 106

CHAPTER 12
Advanced Commands ... 108
Play Dead ... 109
Roll Over ... 109
Crawl ... 110
Spin ... 110
Shake ... 111

CHAPTER 13
Dealing with Unwanted Behaviors ... 112
What Is Bad Behavior in Dogs? ... 113
Finding the Root of the Problem ... 114
Bad Behavior Prevention ... 115
How to Properly Correct Your Dog ... 117
When to Call a Professional ... 119

CHAPTER 14
Traveling with Great Pyrenees ... 120
Crates and Car Restraints ... 121
Preparing Your Dog for Car Rides ... 122
Flying and Hotel Stays ... 123
Kenneling vs. Dog Sitters ... 124
Tips and Tricks for Traveling ... 125

CHAPTER 15
Nutrition ... 128
Importance of a Good Diet ... 128
Good Foods for Great Pyrenees ... 130
Different Types of Commercial Food ... 132
Homemade Foods ... 133
People Foods—Harmful and Acceptable Kinds ... 134
Weight Management ... 135

CHAPTER 16
Grooming Your Great Pyrenees ... 136
Coat Basics ... 137
Bathing ... 138

Trimming Nails ... **140**
Brushing Teeth ... **141**
Cleaning Ears and Eyes ... **142**
When Professional Help Is Necessary ... **143**

CHAPTER 17
Basic Health Care ... **144**
Visiting the Vet ... **145**
Fleas and Ticks ... **146**
Worms and Parasites ... **147**
Common Diseases Found in Great Pyrenees ... **148**
Vaccinations ... **149**
Basics of Senior Dog Care ... **149**
When It's Time to Say Goodbye ... **150**

CHAPTER 1
Great Pyrenees History

What Is a Great Pyrenees?

"I love how instinctual the breed is. They are so smart even though you will hear or read they are stubborn or dumb. I do not consider that accurate. You cannot compare them to a 'domesticated breed'. They are working dogs, and were bred to be self thinkers on their own and to protect. They were not bred to take commands to sit and roll over. They can still be trained and will take commands, but if something requires their attention, they will lock in and you are not easily going to break that focus no matter how loud you yell."

Lindsey Morrison
Golden Pond Farms

Photo Courtesy of Alicia Klocek

CHAPTER 1   Great Pyrenees History

The Great Pyrenees is an internationally recognized dog breed with a long history as a working dog. As the "Great" in the name may hint, this is a big dog with a big personality. This large dog's imposing figure was initially used to guard a flock of sheep from predators. Today, they are more commonly used to protect small children or accompany someone in a wheelchair. Though they are working dogs, they make excellent family companions. However, because of their stubborn temperament, they are best suited for experienced dog owners with lots of patience. Despite this attitude, Great Pyrenees are highly loyal and patient dogs. While their size may be imposing, their personality is not—this is a gentle and loving breed that forms strong bonds with its human family. If you've ever wanted to own your very own cuddly polar bear, this is perhaps the closest you'll get!

History of the Great Pyrenees

Unlike many new and popular crossbreeds, the Great Pyrenees has a long history, and its movement can be traced amongst several continents. While it is difficult to know exactly when the Great Pyrenees became an established breed, there is enough evidence out there to show just how this dog went from a mountain dog to a companion animal.

The name of this breed comes from the Pyrenees Mountains—a mountain range between France and Spain—where this dog was first bred. What is believed to be an early description of this breed was found in writings that date back to the early 1600s, written in Catalan, describing a strong, sturdy wooly cattle dog. Shepherds preferred a guard dog with all-white fur, as it made the dog more visible at dusk and dawn. Any dark patches made it difficult to spot the cattle dog in low light, so an all-white coat came to prominence. The size of this dog was also important when it came to warding off predators. A dog too small would not seem threatening to a wolf that was trying to kill the sheep, while a dog too large would not be agile enough to run after threats. This Great Pyrenees was just the right size to do the very important job of keeping a flock safe.

Later in the seventeenth century, French aristocrats took a liking to the Great Pyrenees. At this time, there was not necessarily a breed standard, as there were two types of Pyrenees dogs. One had a thicker snout and a curlier coat, and the other was sleeker and leaner. Somewhere along the line, some of these traits converged, giving us the Great Pyrenees we know and love today. Dog owners in the 1800s took this breed from the field to the home, liking its calm temperament and stately appearance. Once people began to recognize these good qualities, the Great Pyrenees spread throughout Europe, and overseas to Australia, Canada, and the United States.

In the 1930s, the Great Pyrenees was brought to the United States from France, in an attempt to bring the breed to prominence. In a few short years, the Great Pyrenees was officially recognized by the American Kennel Club. This meant that they were allowed to compete in AKC competitions, as well as creating new standards for which to breed Great Pyrenees pups. While the breed had been brought over the North America earlier in the twentieth century, it wasn't until the 1930s that this breed was officially recognized.

Physical Characteristics

FUN FACT
Great Pyrenees Club of America (GPCA)

The Great Pyrenees Club of America (GPCA) was recognized by the American Kennel Club (AKC) as the official breed club for the Great Pyrenees in 1935. The GPCA is a 501(c)(3) organization, and as part of its efforts to promote and protect the breed, it publishes a club magazine, the GPCA Bulletin. For information on becoming a member of the GPCA, or which services this club provides, visit its website at www.gpcaonline.org.

The Great Pyrenees is a large dog, often compared to other big dogs like the Saint Bernard. At its full adult size, it can weigh anywhere between 80 and 160 pounds, and stands about two and a half feet tall. Female Great Pyrenees tend to weigh 20 pounds less than males, on average. This is a sturdy dog, but it should not be overweight, as the extra fat is hard on the skeletal system. The Great Pyrenees has a medium-length snout and floppy ears. Perhaps the most striking part of this breed's appearance is its thick, fluffy coat. This breed has a double coat, which protects the dog from both cold and hot weather conditions. It sheds a lot, but requires little maintenance apart from regular brushing to keep the coat from getting matted. The coat can range from straight to wavy, but it is rarely curly. Most Great Pyrenees have a solid white coat, though some have tan, gray, or brown markings around their face. The silky coat is especially thick around the neck, and long and feathered on the back of the legs and the tail. Take one look at this dog, and you can imagine its ancestors standing guard over a flock of sheep, or traversing through the rough terrain of the mountains.

CHAPTER 1 Great Pyrenees History

Breed Behavioral Characteristics

"These dogs have the ability to conform to many situations by adapting their inborn traits. They are caregivers, watchers, alarms, uniquely on duty at night, they nap in daytime, like to have a highpoint of vantage to observe, pick up on human's moods and feelings, are compassionate, sweet and understanding of much more than you may realize."

Sharon Reile
Schnee Bar of the Great Plains

The Great Pyrenees makes an excellent family dog because of its friendliness toward people. This dog is extremely loyal, and may adopt young children into its flock to protect. This is an affectionate dog that loves to spend time around its people, so it's important for you to let your dog into areas where you spend most of your time. This dog can handle a range of temperatures, but that doesn't mean that it will enjoy being alone outside all day. The Great Pyrenees will want to watch you as you cook supper and then curl up at the foot of your bed at the end of the day.

Though the large stature of this dog may make you wary about keeping it around children, the Great Pyrenees is generally gentle with children and will enjoy playing with young ones. Of course, all dogs need to be socialized to behave properly around children, and children need to learn how to properly interact with dogs. This will be covered in greater detail in later chapters.

Photo Courtesy of
Beverly Atwood

Erin HOTOVY | The Complete Guide to the Great Pyrenees

Photo Courtesy of Carol Linnell

The only time you may see any unfriendly behaviors with your Great Pyrenees is when strangers come to your door. It isn't that the breed is bad around others, but it often has protective tendencies. Once your dog realizes that a person isn't a threat, he'll warm right up to your visitor. Until then, you can expect barking when someone approaches your front door. Training can help alleviate the dramatic response to visitors, but part of that behavior is in the dog's blood.

If you have other pets, take time to integrate the Great Pyrenees into your home. This breed is generally good with other dogs, so introducing a Great Pyrenees into your pack shouldn't be too stressful. On the other hand, your Great Pyrenees has a high prey drive, so cats and other critters may look like prey to your dog. It isn't impossible to teach your Great Pyrenees to treat your cat like a member of the family, especially at a young age, but be aware that these dogs do like to chase smaller animals.

The Great Pyrenees is fairly intelligent, but has a mind of its own. This is generally not a breed that seeks pleasure from doing tricks and impressing owners with obedience skills. Because of this, you may have a harder time getting your dog to listen to you, compared to more obedient breeds. It's not impossible to obedience train a Great Pyrenees. In fact, it's important to keep a regular training schedule so your dog learns to follow your rules. However, if you're new to dog ownership and training, the Great Pyrenees may test your patience. This dog does well in a home where the owner has a few tricks up their sleeve when it comes to training dogs. Lots of repetition and enticing rewards may convince your Great Pyrenees to listen to you.

CHAPTER 1   Great Pyrenees History

 This breed has a lot of energy and loves to play. Don't let your new dog's size fool you into thinking he's a couch potato—this breed needs plenty of exercise. When you aren't going on long walks, supplement exercise needs with a game of fetch. These dogs love to give chase, so a trip to the dog park with a tennis ball flinger will keep them occupied for a long time. When energetic dogs are left idle, they tend to find ways to get into trouble because they need entertainment. By giving the Great Pyrenees a "job" or a task to complete, your dog will be more likely to behave himself. Also, a tired dog is a good dog. If your Great Pyrenees gets plenty of exercise throughout the day, he'll be less likely to bother you when you need some downtime.

 In general, Great Pyrenees are calm, gentle dogs. They make great workers and great pets. If you're not planning on using them to protect your livestock, they can also find work as support animals because they're great at picking up on their owners' feelings. But if your dog's sole job assignment is to be your new best friend, that's good enough! Your Great Pyrenees will work hard to keep you happy and safe, and you should do the same for him.

Photo Courtesy of Chris and Heather Hendrickson Hendrickson's Circle H Ranch

Is a Great Pyrenees the Right Fit for You?

Before bringing a new dog into your family, it is important to take an honest look at your ability to take care of a Great Pyrenees. This breed is not for everyone, and it saves a lot of stress and heartbreak down the road if you can evaluate your capacity to take care of this breed now, as opposed to trying out the dog and discovering that it's not a good fit for your lifestyle. If you've been eyeing this adorable, fluffy dog for a long time, it can be hard to decide that this may not be an appropriate pet. However, it's important to remember to do what's best for everyone, including the dog. If that means choosing another breed, or waiting until your circumstances can support a Great Pyrenees, then it's necessary to do so.

When deciding if a Great Pyrenees is a good fit for you, first look at your home. If you live in an apartment, it may be hard to raise a Great Pyrenees. For starters, this is a big, energetic dog that needs a lot of space to move around. If left in an apartment for too long, a Great Pyrenees may feel cooped up and find destructive ways to entertain himself. Also, these dogs have extremely good hearing and like to warn their owners if someone is approaching the home. Guard duty doesn't end at night, either. If people are entering and exiting the apartment building at all hours, your dog will keep barking. Owning a dog that barks a lot in an apartment is an easy way to upset your neighbors and draw noise complaints. A home with a fenced-in yard is best for the Great Pyrenees. A fence around the yard is essential for this breed, as it likes to escape and roam around.

Next, think about your training expectations for your dream dog. Do you want a dog that can show off a bunch of fun tricks? The Great Pyrenees is notoriously challenging to train. This breed is intelligent, but was bred to do a specific task. If your commands fall outside of what your dog thinks is necessary to complete a job, he's less likely to obey. The breed has a mind of its own, and training Great Pyrenees therefore requires some knowledge and patience. If you're cool and collected, have some training skills, and don't mind if your dog never learns how to roll over, then this dog will work for you. If you had dreams of entering your dog in agility contests, have little time and patience, and don't feel comfortable with your training skills, this breed may prove to be too much for you.

Along with having the mental energy to train this dog, you will also need physical energy and time. If you hate going on long walks or throwing a ball around the dog park for an hour, you might prefer a dog with fewer exercise requirements. The Great Pyrenees is an energetic dog that may become destructive and gain excess weight if he isn't allowed to burn off some of his energy. If you have physical limitations that make it difficult to go on long walks, have little extra time for taking your dog on adventures, or would prefer to stay inside, then the Great Pyrenees may not be a good fit. On the other hand, if you love to spend time outside regardless of the weather, enjoy being active, and can devote a couple hours a day to your dog's exercise needs, then the Great Pyrenees will make an excellent addition to your daily exercise routine.

Next, consider how a Great Pyrenees will affect your home. If someone in your household is allergic to dog dander, a Great Pyrenees may aggravate allergies because of how much the breed sheds. Likewise, if you dislike having pet fur in your home and all over your clothes, you may prefer a breed that doesn't shed so much. Also, if you cannot tolerate barking and howling, the Great Pyrenees isn't for you. But if you don't mind a little noise and a little mess, the Great Pyrenees might make a great companion.

Finally, consider the time and money required to have this breed in your home. Because feeding is often based on body weight, a Great Pyrenees will eat much more kibble than a ten-pound dog. Over time, the cost of food adds up. Also, this breed loves to be around people and will become unhappy if left in isolation for too long. In general, dogs require a lot of money and attention to give them the life they deserve. If you know you don't have your finances in order or you have a lot of other time-consuming things going on in your life, it may be wise to revisit dog ownership at a more stable time.

If you feel like you might be a good owner for a Great Pyrenees, read on! The following chapters will give you the tips and tricks you need for raising a happy and healthy pup. Bringing a new dog into your household is a big life change, so it's important to have all the resources you need and all the information you can take in.

The Great Pyrenees is a unique dog with a long history. Though the Great Pyrenees of today make great house pets, they still have their working dog spirit. This is a dog that needs a job—as the owner, it's your task to find the right job for your pup! Whether you train your dog to protect your flock, provide emotional support, or just to give you cuddles, you'll have a great time finding ways to keep your dog healthy and happy. In return, your dog will give you ample love and happiness.

CHAPTER 2
Choosing a Great Pyrenees

Once you decide the Great Pyrenees is the right breed for you, it's time to pick out your new best friend! Because you'll have your little buddy by your side for his entire life, you'll want to make sure you pick out the best pup for you. This process isn't as simple as picking out a picture of a dog on the Internet, or going to a pet store. If you want the right dog, you need to do some research. This chapter will walk you through the steps of picking out your first Great Pyrenees.

Photo Courtesy of Lisa Woods

CHAPTER 2   Choosing a Great Pyrenees

Buying vs. Adopting

The first decision you need to make is whether you want to purchase a puppy from a breeder or adopt a Great Pyrenees from a shelter or rescue. There are pros and cons to both options, so it's important to take your personal wants and values into consideration before making a choice. There is no wrong option so long as you're making an informed decision based on what you want or need for your household.

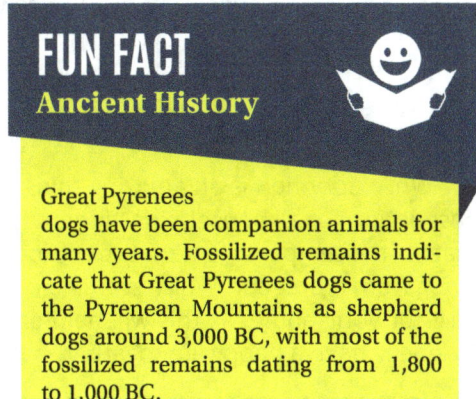

FUN FACT
Ancient History

Great Pyrenees dogs have been companion animals for many years. Fossilized remains indicate that Great Pyrenees dogs came to the Pyrenean Mountains as shepherd dogs around 3,000 BC, with most of the fossilized remains dating from 1,800 to 1,000 BC.

Buying a puppy from a reputable breeder is a good option if you want to know exactly what you're getting in a Great Pyrenees. A good breeder can provide you with a purebred dog, bred to national standards. Also, well-bred dogs often come with health guarantees so you know they won't be likely to suffer from genetic ailments later in life.

Many dog owners prefer to bring a puppy into their home, as opposed to an adult Great Pyrenees. For starters, if you bring a puppy home straight from the breeder, you know that you're its first owner. That means that your dog hasn't been exposed to any training (or lack of training) yet. This fresh start might be nice if you plan on having strict rules in your home and don't want to bring home an adult that has bad habits. Also, you can be sure that the puppy has been treated well and hasn't experienced anything traumatic when you buy from a good breeder. If you have very specific hopes and plans for your new Great Pyrenees, a new puppy from a good breeder is the way to go. The right puppy from a good breeder should have all of the good qualities people love about Great Pyrenees, with fewer of the temperamental problems and health concerns found in poorly bred dogs.

On the other hand, adopting a dog from a shelter or Great Pyrenees rescue is a rewarding experience. When you adopt, you're giving a good home to a dog in need. Oftentimes, a dog is surrendered because their human was not able to take care of it, at no fault of the dog's. Other times, the dog was surrendered because it had a trait that was incompatible to the family's lifestyle, like a dog that was too intimidating or scary in a home full of children. These are still wonderful dogs if your home is a good match for them.

Another benefit of adoption is the option of bringing home an adult dog. While puppies are adorable, they are a ton of work. Imagine getting to own a Great Pyrenees without having to potty train and deal with puppy teeth marks in all of your belongings! Sometimes a rescue dog will already know basic commands and have some socialization skills. As an added bonus, dog rescues charge a fraction of what a puppy costs, so you can spend your puppy budget on fun toys and treats!

While adoption is an amazing thing to do for a dog in need, it's not the best option for all households. If there is not an available dog at the shelter that fits the temperament that you're looking for, you may want to purchase a dog from a breeder. Whichever choice you make, remember to do what's best for your home, as this will help ensure that you and your new Great Pyrenees have a happy life together.

CHAPTER 2   Choosing a Great Pyrenees

How to Find a Reputable Breeder

When buying a puppy, it's vital that you find a reputable Great Pyrenees breeder for multiple reasons. For starters, poorly bred dogs can come with a multitude of health and behavioral issues. The last thing you want to do after spending a bunch of money on a dog is to then also have to spend a lot of money on health care for a sick pup. Another reason you want to buy from the right person is because you don't want to support a puppy mill or any other unethical breeding operation. Give your support to a breeder with a vast knowledge, a lot of enthusiasm for the Great Pyrenees breed, and who uses best breeding practices and cares about the well-being of their pups.

Unfortunately, there are a lot of breeders who breed dogs as a way to make some extra money. While anyone can buy a male and a female Great Pyrenees and sell their puppies, a talented breeder can pick the best dogs to yield a litter with all of the best characteristics and avoid genetic diseases. Bad or merely inexperienced breeders may seem to have the best intentions, while breeding dogs that will later display unwanted traits, like aggression or fearfulness. The worst of the "backyard breeders" are the ones who only want to capitalize on dog trends and treat their dogs poorly. Not only are these pups carelessly bred, but they are often kept in small, dirty conditions unsuitable for any living creature.

There are certainly clues to look for when finding the right breeder that will tell you if a breeder is reputable or just a backyard breeder. Price is often the first hint. If a puppy is being offered at a price that seems too good to be true, it probably is. Be wary of sellers asking for prices much lower than average. While the price of some dogs seems high, it's because a lot of time, money, and expertise goes into breeding a good dog. If you're buying a pup to work for you, it's okay to pay top dollar for a superior product.

Next, choose a breeder that is willing to let you meet the pups and see their business. Because most breeders work out of their home, it's important to be respectful of visiting times. However, if a breeder is willing to show you the pups and the dogs they use for breeding, it can tell you a lot about the puppies they produce. If the facilities where the dogs are kept are clean, spacious, and comfortable, that's a good clue that a breeder takes good care of their dogs. If the dogs used for breeding are friendly, relaxed, and playful, you'll be more likely to end up with a pup with those same qualities. If your breeder's home sets off any red flags, you probably want to go elsewhere to obtain your puppy. Cramped quarters, dirty living conditions, and sickly dogs are all signs that the breeder does not care about the overall well-being of the pups.

A conversation with a breeder about their Great Pyrenees can also be telling. If the breeder is unable to answer basic questions about the breed, they may be in the business for the money, and not for the love of the breed. But if your breeder has lots of good information about the breed and asks you questions about your ability to take care of one of their pups, you know that this person has the knowledge and care necessary to be a good breeder.

Photo Courtesy of Alicia Klocek

CHAPTER 2 Choosing a Great Pyrenees

Researching Breeders

> *"The biggest thing that I look for with breeders are: AKC registration with full registration rights, and do they OFA test their adults. It's also important that when you talk to them they tell you the full story on their dogs and puppies, the breeds good, bad or ugly and not just the sugar coated version of what you want to hear in order to make the sale."*
>
> ***Lindsey Morrison***
> *Golden Pond Farms*

When you know what you're looking for in a breeder, it's time to do some research. This can be a time-consuming process if you're starting from scratch, but you'll be glad you did the proper vetting when you have your new best friend at home. If you know you want a Great Pyrenees and have no idea where to find one, here are a few ways to start your search.

If you know someone with a Great Pyrenees, ask where they bought their pup. Or, if you know trainers, veterinarians, or other people who work with dogs, ask if they know any breeders. A referral from a friend or acquaintance can narrow your search in a hurry. You'll be able to hear firsthand about the health and temperament of a particular breeder's pups, plus you will learn about the experience of buying from that particular breeder.

If you don't have any connections to a breeder, then you will probably start with a general Internet search. Once you find a few breeders, do some research on social media. Many breeders have business pages with client reviews. Here, you can learn about the breeders, see any qualifications they may have, and see what other people have to say about their puppies. Be wary of breeders who give few details about their operations, or people who only sell in the classified ads without a website or other information to show their credibility. Not all reputable breeders may have a fancy website or big social media following, but if the breeder has taken the time to advertise their Great Pyrenees breeding business, there's a good chance they care about the breed, and not just about making money.

Once you've narrowed your list of breeders down, get in contact with the breeder. If you send them a friendly email or call with questions about the breed, they should respond within a reasonable timeframe. Generally, dog breeders enjoy sharing their knowledge and love of a breed with potential dog owners. If you find that you really enjoy talking with a particular person, this may be your breeder! Your relationship with this person doesn't have to end when you buy your dog. Many breeders love to hear updates about their pups and offer advice to their clients. You want to give your business to someone you feel comfortable speaking to, as a breeder can be a fantastic resource to use throughout your dog's life. A trustworthy breeder will also be happy to give you references to vouch for their reliability as a Great Pyrenees breeder. All in all, you should feel comfortable around your breeder. If you see any red flags during this vetting process, find a different breeder you can trust.

Health Tests and Certifications

A reputable breeder cares about the health of their Great Pyrenees and does whatever they can to avoid breeding pups with genetic illnesses or other health problems. Disorders of the skeletal system are more common in very large dogs because they grow so quickly, so it's important for the parents of your puppy to be in good health, in order for your pup to have a better chance of avoiding future health problems. According to breeder Susan Grimm of Grimm Acres, Diversified, Great Pyrenees dogs can be X-rayed for signs of hip dysplasia at one year old. So, if your breeder tests their dogs for signs of hip dysplasia, you'll have a better chance of ending up with a healthy pup than if you buy from a breeder who doesn't test their dogs at all.

With this type of testing, your breeder may have some sort of documentation from a veterinarian that shows these results. Don't be afraid to ask your breeder for any proof of health tests, or even for the name of the veterinarian they use. A reputable breeder should be transparent with the claims they make about the health of their dogs.

Along with health tests from a vet, ask your breeder about any kind of kennel club membership or certification. If a breeder is truly passionate about Great Pyrenees, they will likely have some sort of involvement with a breed-specific organization. Many breeders pay a lot of money for dogs with excellent lineage and may even have certificates that prove that their dogs have come from a long line of champions. Your breeder will probably make this information available to you before you even ask, as they'll be so proud of the good work they do.

CHAPTER 2   Choosing a Great Pyrenees

Breeder Contracts and Guarantees

Another thing you may want to ask your breeder about is any sort of contract or guarantee that releases liability of the breeder or owner. Sometimes, a breeder will request that the new owner take their pup to the vet for a checkup within a month or so after purchase. This is to ensure that the puppy is in good health so the owner cannot dispute the breeder's reliability if something happens to the puppy in the future. At the same time, this checkup protects the owner if a vet finds something wrong early on, so the responsibility for health care does not rest solely on the new owner. A good breeder does not want to sell a sick dog to a potential Great Pyrenees owner, so the breeder should be in no great hurry to make a sale and sever ties with the owner. And, in the event of an unforeseen circumstance where things do not work out with your puppy in the early days, you may lose the deposit, but there's a chance the breeder will be willing to give you a partial refund and re-home the dog for you.

Choosing the Perfect Pup

"I always choose my Pyre by looking them in the face. Your Pyrenees should gaze back at you holding eye contact. They should look at you as though they're reading your mind which is in fact one of the great things about Pyrenees. Pyrenees want to read your mind and they want to do what makes you happy."

Susan Grimm
Grimm Acres, Diversified

Once you've found your breeder, it's time to pick out your new puppy. Oftentimes, this process turns into choosing the cutest pup from a photo online instead of actually meeting the dogs. Physically choosing your puppy is better because you cannot learn about a pup's temperament from a photo. Yes, appearance may be important in your decision, but your new dog's personality will ultimately make the most difference in your mutual happiness.

When making your pick from the litter, you want a dog that's curious, but not overbearing. A dog that's playful, but not too aggressive will grow up to be relaxed, but fun. While a shy and skittish puppy may be less rambunctious than the others, fearfulness is not a desirable quality in an adult dog. Many times, it's best to choose the dog that is in the middle of the extremes in the litter. Some prospective owners like to meet all of the pups to see which one they feel the strongest connection to. While this method won't necessarily tell you how your pup will act as an adult, it's important to feel like you have a connection to your new dog. Oftentimes, people like the dog that "chooses them."

If you've been talking to a breeder for a while, you may have to put a deposit down on a pup before you can take them home. Puppies need to have enough time with their mother and siblings before they can be brought home. While it can be hard to wait, this is done in your pup's best interest. Spend the time between picking out your pup and bringing them home preparing for your new arrival.

"It depends on if you are looking for: a working dog or a house dog. The more hyper active playful puppies tend to make better house pets and playmates to children, and the calmer ones tend to be easier to train as working dogs, in my opinion."

Lindsey Morrison
Golden Pond Farms

CHAPTER 2 Choosing a Great Pyrenees

Photo Courtesy of Breanna Fortner

Tips for Adopting a Great Pyrenees

"If you are looking for a family companion start with a rescue. Like any other breed there are many wonderful Great Pyrenees that have been given up to rescue for different reasons. The rescue organization you choose to work with should be, as most of them are, open and transparent. The staff should know the dogs well enough to talk to you about the dog's personality and traits. Most do an excellent job of health screening and vet care."

Susan Grimm
Grimm Acres, Diversified

If you've decided to go through the adoption process, prepare for a screening process. Shelters and rescues are looking for the best homes possible for their dogs, so they need to be convinced that you can take care of one of their Great Pyrenees before they release their dog to you. An application form will ask questions about your home, the people who live there, and what your daily schedule is like. If your application goes through, someone will likely visit your home to make sure your fence is secure enough for a Great Pyrenees and check for any other red flags that might prevent a Great Pyrenees from doing well in your home.

A general animal shelter's screening process will probably be less involved than a Great Pyrenees rescue's process because the rescue knows the breed on a more intimate level than a shelter that deals with tons of different dogs. Rescues are typically smaller, so you may find that they try to match you with a particular dog based on your life circumstances, as opposed to letting you choose one from their rescue. These dogs generally go through a foster process so the rescue knows what kind of a home would suit them the best. For example, if you have other dogs in your home, but the dog that catches your eye at the rescue would be best as an only dog, the rescue will probably not let you adopt that particular dog.

When you go to the shelter to pick out a dog, plan on making multiple visits with anyone in your household. You want to see how the dog reacts around adults, children, and other pets. If these meetings go well, you're ready for an in-home trial. Plan to let the dog spend the day at your house and see how he does in his new surroundings. Some rescues will release their dogs on a trial basis and check in on you to see how things are going.

CHAPTER 2   Choosing a Great Pyrenees

If the relationship between dog and prospective owner is going well after a month or so, the rescue will officially release the dog into your care.

Try to learn as much as possible about your shelter dog. While many dogs that are surrendered are great dogs and do well in all sorts of homes, some may be surrendered because they don't do well in certain circumstances. If you know more about the dogs, you'll have a better idea of which dogs will do the best in your particular home situation.

Once you decide you want a Great Pyrenees, it can be hard to wait for the right dog to come to you. However, it's important not to rush the adoption process. If you bring home the first Great Pyrenees that's available in your area, you may find that the dog doesn't work well in your home. Or, if you rush through meeting the dog and getting him acclimated into your home, you may not see potential issues or could overwhelm the dog. It can be exciting to get a new dog, but it's good make sure everyone is happy before making a permanent decision.

The process of getting a new Great Pyrenees is exciting, but remember to take your time when looking for a breeder or rescue dog. There are lots of ways to obtain a Great Pyrenees, but you want to make sure you're getting the best dog for your home while supporting ethical breeding practices. If you do your research to find the best breeder in your area, you'll be better off than if you bought the first dog you found in the classifieds page. It can be hard to find a reputable breeder when there are so many breeders out there, but with some research and patience, you'll find a great resource you can use long after you purchase your new pup!

CHAPTER 3

Preparing Your Home for Your Great Pyrenees

The arrival of a new dog can be stressful if not enough preparation is done before you bring your pup home. Puppies are mischievous creatures that like to get into trouble and make messes. They're also a member of the family that will want to have their own space to feel safe and comfortable. Before your new dog places its paws in your home, make sure to get your home ready for your new dog. That way, you can spend your first days bonding with your pup instead of frantically trying to puppy-proof your home.

Photo Courtesy of Becca Ylitalo

CHAPTER 3   Preparing Your Home for Your Great Pyrenees

Adjusting Your Current Pets and Children

Perhaps the most important thing you can do to make your new dog's transition to your home a successful one is to prepare your pets and kids for the new puppy. The Great Pyrenees is generally very good with other dogs and children, but this doesn't mean that they will always respond positively to other dogs and children. Young puppies lack the socialization skills needed to interact with other dogs. A puppy's misstep may cause an adult dog to put them in their place. This isn't necessarily a bad thing, but it's best to avoid squabbles whenever possible.

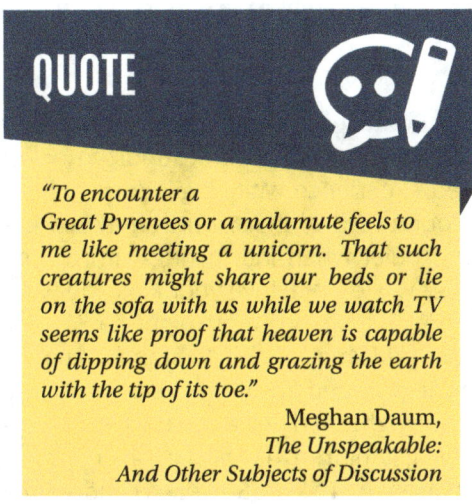

QUOTE

"To encounter a Great Pyrenees or a malamute feels to me like meeting a unicorn. That such creatures might share our beds or lie on the sofa with us while we watch TV seems like proof that heaven is capable of dipping down and grazing the earth with the tip of its toe."

Meghan Daum,
The Unspeakable: And Other Subjects of Discussion

If your existing dog is well-socialized and good with other dogs, then you probably won't have too much of a problem adding another dog to the pack. Still, it's a good idea to have your new dog and old dog meet before bringing your new puppy home for good. Ideally, this first meeting would take place in a safe, neutral place, like a friend's backyard. This way, neither dog will feel territorial over the space. Have a friend or family member take one dog's leash while you take the other. That way, if things get out of hand, you'll have quick control over the dogs. Allow your pups to sniff and greet each other. Don't force them to play if they're not interested in being in close corners. As long as neither dog is afraid or unfriendly to the other, then you can call your first meeting a success. If possible, have your dogs meet a few more times in your home under close supervision to ensure that your dogs feel comfortable around each other. If your existing dog is not up to date on his shots, make sure you take care of that before bringing a vulnerable puppy into the picture. You don't want your new puppy to get sick before he's received all of his vaccinations.

Cats or other non-canine pets may create issues for your Great Pyrenees because this breed has a moderate prey drive. This means that they will see your little cat and have the urge to chase after it. If your puppy is still young and impressionable, you may have more success with teaching him to leave your cat alone. If you adopted a dog that isn't used to being around cats, you may have a challenge when teaching him not to chase your cat. On the other hand, it's possible to adopt a dog that has prior experience with cats and who gets along well with felines. Regardless of your dog's behavior around cats, make sure there is always an escape plan for your kitty. A cat tree or easy access to dog-free rooms will prevent your dog and cat from getting into altercations.

Because children can (sometimes) be reasoned with, talk with them about how to behave around the new puppy, especially if they have limited experience with dogs. Young children naturally become very excited around cute animals, which may scare a dog. Remind your kids to be calm and quiet when interacting with the puppy. Over time, your Great Pyrenees will learn to love your kids and will enjoy running around the yard with them, but a new puppy might not know what to make of noisy people. Also, some kids may not understand that a dog doesn't like to have his tail pulled or be prodded around his ears, nose, eyes, and mouth. If a dog gets especially frightened or aggravated, it may snap at the child. As a result, the child may get injured, develop an aversion to dogs, and your dog might develop an aversion to kids. So, teach children how to pet a dog nicely. Instruct them to gently stroke the dog's back, avoiding the face altogether, just to be safe. As your dog gets to know the kids, he'll become more comfortable having little children hanging all over him.

Photo Courtesy of Leslie Mori

CHAPTER 3   Preparing Your Home for Your Great Pyrenees

Dangerous Things that Dogs Might Eat

Adult Great Pyrenees are tall enough to reach tables and countertops with ease. This breed likes to overeat, so your dog may finish his dinner and move onto whatever is lying around for dessert. Especially in the early days when your dog doesn't know how to behave in your home, keep everything out of reach. If you don't want something to go in your dog's mouth, don't leave it somewhere accessible.

Be mindful of the plants you keep inside and outside the home. While many are safe for dogs to ingest, many can make a dog very ill.

Common culprits are:
- Hostas
- Several variations of ivy
- Poinsettias
- Different types of lilies

Because there are many plants out there with various levels of toxicity, it would be wise to do some research on the plants you keep in and around your home and figure out if any are a danger to your dog. If you have toxic plants, it doesn't necessarily mean that you need to tear up your entire yard. Instead, keep an eye on your pup while they're playing in the yard. If you see them try to take a nibble of a plant that may make them sick, then take the necessary precautions. Also, when it comes to toxic foods, a tiny taste of a plant probably won't doom your dog, as the Great Pyrenees is a giant breed. However, if your dog is still a puppy or ingests a lot of something they shouldn't, a trip to the vet is likely the best move. If you have dangerous plants in the house, either place the plant out of reach, like in a hanging basket, or in a room you keep off-limits to your pup.

Not all human foods are safe for your dog to eat, either. In fact, there are foods humans eat on a regular basis that can make a dog extremely ill if too much is ingested. Here are a few common human foods that can make a dog sick:
- Cooked bones can splinter when chewed and shards can be lodged in a dog's mouth or digestive system.
- Chocolate, coffee, and other caffeinated foods and beverages can cause vomiting and diarrhea, panting, seizures, and abnormal heart rhythm.
- Grapes and raisins can cause kidney failure.
- Milk and other types of dairy are not dangerous for dogs, but it can give them digestive distress because they lack the enzymes necessary to break down cow's milk.

- Onions can cause red blood cell damage if ingested in significant amounts.
- Xylitol is an artificial sweetener found in a lot of processed foods that can cause insulin release, which can lead to low blood sugar and liver failure
- Macadamia nuts can cause weakness, vomiting, tremors, and even hyperthermia in dogs.

Even inorganic materials can become a hazard if ingested. Dogs will gulp up anything within reach, like spare change, socks, and whatever they can find in the garbage. Oftentimes, these household items will pass through without incident. However, if the object is large enough, it can become a choking hazard. Or, if there is enough of the material in your dog's digestive tract, it can create an internal obstruction that will have to be surgically removed. Dogs can be very quick and sneaky when they gobble your household items, so be extra careful not to leave your belongings within reach.

Photo Courtesy of Courtney Martinez

CHAPTER 3 Preparing Your Home for Your Great Pyrenees

Other Household Dangers

Puppies are known for chewing on everything they can find, as it's an entertaining activity and can feel good on sore puppy teeth. An electrical cord may look like a chewy rope to a dog but can cause shocks, burns, and can potentially electrocute a dog. Be sure to keep cords out of reach and safely secured so a dog cannot nibble on one.

Photo Courtesy of Marissa Manning

Because of this dog's size, you may want to take a look at your furniture and make sure a dog can't tip it over onto himself. Plant stands, bookshelves, and end tables may fall over if your dog tries to jump up to investigate whatever objects are on top. Also, it's important to remember that household objects are not necessarily safe if they're placed up off of the floor. If a Great Pyrenees finds something enticing on the table, it won't be long until your puppy is big enough to jump up and grab it.

Cleaning chemicals can make your dog seriously ill if they are ingested. While cleaning supplies stowed up high in secure cabinets are usually safe, never underestimate a dog's ability to nose into eye-level cupboards. If you catch your pup snooping around your cupboards, you may want to invest in some child safety locks. Also, some dogs can't resist lapping up toilet water. As toilets are often cleaned with harsh chemicals or use treated water, this can make your dog very sick. Close the toilet lid—and maybe the bathroom door—to keep your dog from drinking chemicals. If your dog has access to your garage or garden, make sure pesticides and fertilizers are stored out of reach.

Photo Courtesy of Shelby Brewer

CHAPTER 3   Preparing Your Home for Your Great Pyrenees

Preparing Indoor Spaces

"Remember that they are chewers. Keep all shoes up and important things off the ground. Have things that they can chew on like toys always available. If they do chew on something, tell them no and give them something they are allowed to chew on. Depending on the dog, furniture might even be gnawed on the corners, so be aware when they are left alone."

Lindsey Morrison
Golden Pond Farms

Along with removing anything that can be a hazard or unintended chew toy for your dog, you need to make sure your little one feels welcome and safe in your home. Puppies are notoriously messy, so many new owners like to set up a small area for their dog on a floor that can be easily cleaned. Then, this area can be sectioned off with a dog pen or several baby gates that block off prohibited areas of the house. A puppy won't mind the smaller quarters, but an adult Great Pyrenees will need a little more room to roam. However, with good training, your adult dog will not make too much of a mess around your home.

Every dog needs a cozy spot where he can feel safe in your home. For some owners, this is a crate that is placed in an area where people spend the majority of their time. A corner of the kitchen or living room is a good setup for a dog. Great Pyrenees like to spend time around their human family, so you definitely don't want to place them in an isolated part of the house, like a laundry room or basement. A dog bed also makes a comfy hangout for your pooch if you choose not to crate train (this is discussed later in the book).

If your new Great Pyrenees is not potty trained, you will probably want to protect your floors. A kitchen is a good home base for a dog because the floors are generally easier to clean than a carpeted room. Still, you'll want to put down some newspaper or puppy pads to make cleaning easier. You can expect to have plenty of accidents on the floor in the first few weeks, so anything you can do to make cleaning easier will help you focus your time on your dog, and not your floors.

Also, when it comes to cleaning up after your dog, remember that Great Pyrenees are heavy shedders. If you want to keep your couches and bed clear of pet fur, either prohibit these spaces to your dog, or cover them in a protective blanket. A good vacuum and lint rollers are also great to keep on hand. Or, you can just embrace the double coat and let the fur fly freely!

Preparing Outdoor Spaces

Great Pyrenees absolutely love being outside in cool temperatures. Their thick coat helps them stay warm when most dogs want to curl up inside. Their special coat also keeps them comfortable in summer months, though they need to take it easy when it's hot. These dogs do well in a backyard with a tall and sturdy fence. They need plenty of time in the fresh air to patrol your outdoor space and play. Because it's hard to give your dog your full attention at all times, you'll want to make sure your backyard is just as comfortable as your dog's indoor spot.

The most important thing you need in your yard is a sturdy fence. Great Pyrenees can be escape artists and wander far beyond your property if given the opportunity. A six-foot fence works well to keep your dog from peeking over and finding a way to jump out of your yard. Many owners like wooden or plastic fences that keep dogs from seeing everything outside the yard. These dogs in particular like to play watchdog, so limiting the stimuli in your immediate area may cut down on the warning barks. You'll also want to make sure that your dog will not be able to dig underneath the fence and escape. And, while some dog owners can get away with chaining their dog up for a short amount of time in lieu of a fence, a Great Pyrenees is much too strong to do this safely. It only takes one rabbit to cause your dog to break through the collar or tether. To keep your dog safe, keep him enclosed in an area that he cannot escape.

Along with removing dangerous plants that your dog likes to nibble on, look for anything else that can cause a dog harm. For example, some dogs like to chew on rocks found in the yard, which can crack teeth and cause internal obstructions. Or, a child's toys, if forgotten outside, can be chewed and devoured. Take a little time to make sure there's nothing in your backyard that can become hazardous to your new dog.

If your new dog insists on spending as much time outside as possible, it may be nice to give him a doghouse or an umbrella or awning to shelter from the elements. However, don't forget that these dogs love companionship, so also bring your dog inside so he can spend time with you. This breed loves to spend time outside, but does not want to be banished to a space away from people.

When your home is ready for a new family member, you'll have even more time to focus on your new pet. In the days and weeks leading up to your dog's arrival, spend a little time each day making your home a safe and welcoming place for a new dog. This process is not un-

CHAPTER 3   Preparing Your Home for Your Great Pyrenees

like baby-proofing a house, as you'll want to think like a dog and look for anything that can harm your pup. It's also important to slowly introduce your new dog to any pets or children in your home so you don't have to worry about issues arising once your dog has started to settle into their new home. The early days of dog care are a lot of work, so save yourself as much stress as possible and make sure your home is in order before you add a new pup to the mix.

CHAPTER 4
Bringing Your Great Pyrenees Home

After lots of research and waiting, it's finally time to bring your new dog home! This is an exciting time for a new dog owner. Because the first few days will likely be a bit hectic, this chapter should serve as a checklist of sorts to help you get the important tasks completed, while still having plenty of time to enjoy your new Great Pyrenees.

Photo Courtesy of Amber M Lecy

The Importance of Having a Plan

A new dog presents a lot of new challenges. Puppies that are not housetrained make a lot of messes and require frequent trips outside. Puppies are cute, but they have a hard time sleeping through the night and demand a lot of attention to make sure they're not doing something dangerous or destructive. Meanwhile, lots of people are going to want to see your new dog, and you'll want to introduce your dog to your friends and family. You'll also have to gather supplies, find a vet, and figure out how you're going to pay for it all.

It's easy to get caught up in the excitement of having a new dog, then realize several months later that you forgot to sign up for the puppy class and all of the spots are now full. So a loose plan, even if it's just in your head, can be extremely helpful for getting through the chaos that is life with a new dog. That way, you can enjoy your time with your puppy and set them up for the best life ever. What follows is a discussion of a possible plan to make this as easy as possible.

The Ride Home

To make the trip from the breeder or shelter to your home easier, it's nice to have someone accompany you on your trip to pick up your new dog. It can be very distracting to have a dog in your car in general, but especially so if you're trying to ensure that your new dog is handling the trip well. This is likely the first time your dog has ever been separated from his family, so he's bound to be a little apprehensive. Having a driver allows you to hold your new dog, or sit beside his crate and speak in a soothing voice on your trip home. Safety restraints will become necessary for car trips in later days, but if you need to cuddle your little one for his first ride away from his family, it may help him feel more comfortable.

It's not uncommon for dogs to get carsick, especially if they aren't used to riding in vehicles or are already nervous. Before you go to pick up your new dog, stash a few old towels in your car, just in case you need to clean up any messes. You may also want to bring a few treats with you in order to make your dog feel more comfortable around you. Treats let your dog know that everything is okay, and will likely make positive associations with car rides (and you) so they're less nervous the next time you go for a ride.

If you're making a long trip to pick up your new pup, you'll have to take hotels and flying into consideration, as both can cause stress on a dog. Chapter 14 has some tips and tricks for making that part of your trip as smooth as possible.

Photo Courtesy of Alicia Klocek

The First Night Home

With so much excitement, your new dog will probably be absolutely exhausted by the end of his first day at home. If you're lucky, this may mean that he will sleep hard for a while. But more likely than not, your dog will probably spend a good portion of the night crying and restless. There are a few reasons why your dog is preventing you from getting sleep.

First of all, dogs don't keep the same sleep schedule as humans. While we tend to stay up all day and sleep for a long stretch at night, dogs sleep off and on throughout the day. A dog might go to bed when you do, but he'll be wide awake a couple hours later. This is especially apparent in the Great Pyrenees because this breed is hardwired to look out for their flock. So, while you rest, your dog may think it's his job to look out for the family while they're in a vulnerable state.

Puppies also cry at night because they have to go to the bathroom and that's the only way they can tell you that they need to be let out. A puppy bladder is too small to hold the urge to potty for more than an hour or so. So, if your dog is alerting you that he's about to have an accident, he will cry as a way to get your attention. Taking your dog out right before going to bed and limiting water within an hour of bedtime may keep your dog from need-

CHAPTER 4 *Bringing Your Great Pyrenees Home*

ing to go all night. However, be careful with how you limit your dog's access to fresh water, as he can become dehydrated.

Finally, your new dog is probably crying because he's scared or lonely. It's hard for a dog to go from spending all of his time with his mother and siblings in the place they were born, to sleeping in an unfamiliar place with unfamiliar people. Even if you've adopted an adult dog, the transition to a new home is jarring and may make it difficult for a dog to relax enough to sleep. To minimize these negative feelings, place your dog in a spot where he can see, hear, or smell you. This works well if your dog is in a crate, because you can simply place the crate near your bed and not have to worry about being disturbed by a wandering dog. You can also let your dog sleep on your bed, but don't let your five-pound puppy do anything you wouldn't let your hundred-pound adult dog do.

Your dog will grow out of this stage with time. Until then, make sure you take your pup to go potty right before bed and give him plenty of exercise throughout the day so he's positively pooped at night. Before long, your dog will keep a quiet watch over you at night without bothering you with intermittent whining.

Photo Courtesy of Melanie Hollingworth

What to Expect in the First Few Weeks

Being a puppy parent is exhausting. Not only do you have to look out for your little one and make sure he's taken care of, but you also need to keep him from wreaking havoc in your home. Puppies' tiny bladders will cause them to have accidents on a daily basis, even if you're vigilant about taking them out on a regular schedule. They will want to explore everything, which involves putting everything they find in their mouth.

While you're cleaning up after your little monster, you're also attempting to teach your puppy how to live in your household. It's never too early to start working on good behavior and correcting bad behavior before it turns into a habit. However, the most effective way to reward or correct behaviors is by catching your dog in the act. So, in between cleaning up messes, you'll need to keep a close eye on your dog to make sure that he's behaving appropriately. This breed needs plenty of love and attention, so they'll probably follow you around the house, just because they want to hang out with you. However, new dogs can get overwhelmed by too much excitement. New dog owners often like to show their new pup to their friends and family. This is a time where your dog is trying to adjust to living in a new home with new people, and too many strangers can upset your dog. So, while it's great to have visitors see your dog in the early days, try to give your dog some time alone to relax. Never force your dog to interact if he isn't feeling up to it.

Photo Courtesy of Melanie Hollingworth

CHAPTER 4   Bringing Your Great Pyrenees Home

Overall, you can expect to spend most of your free time taking care of your pup in the early days. While this can be exhausting and you'll wonder what you got yourself into, remember that your dog will soon be an adult and will no longer need the constant attention. Cherish the time you have with your puppy because it's fun to watch him learn and grow.

The First Vet Visit

Early on in your puppy's life, he will need to go to the vet. It's important to establish a relationship with a vet in the early days so you can ensure that your dog is up to date on vaccines and disease-free. Oftentimes, puppies acquire worms. Also, your breeder may insist that you see a vet so they can confirm that your dog is in good health, releasing liability of their responsibilities as a breeder. Either way, it's a good idea to find a new vet and have them look over your new dog to make sure your new pup is healthy.

If you don't already have a vet, take a little time to find one that you like. Keep in mind that there are different types of clinics with different kinds of facilities. Some vets have simple offices that allow them to examine animals and treat minor ailments. These vets may have the ability to take samples from your dog, but lack the laboratory to return immediate results. Some offices have a lab, but do not offer emergency services or have capabilities to perform major surgery. And some have quite extensive facilities and can perform just about every test and procedure necessary. If you choose a vet that doesn't have someone on-call for emergencies, it's wise to have the phone number and address of an emergency vet on hand, just in case.

If you don't have a local vet, ask your breeder or local dog shelter who they use. A local Great Pyrenees breeder is a great source of information because they can vouch for their vet's knowledge of the breed. You can also ask friends and acquaintances for a veterinary clinic reference. You're turning over your dog's health to the veterinarian, so you'll want to make sure you truly trust this person. A good vet listens to your concerns about your pet and takes the time to explain everything you need to know about your dog's health.

Dogs get nervous about going to the vet because there are so many new sights, smells, and sensations. It's normal for your dog to be a little apprehensive about seeing the vet. But it is much easier for your vet to complete an examination if your dog is calm. To set your dog up for success, it's important for you to stay relaxed. Great Pyrenees are sensitive dogs that pick up on the emotions of their humans. If your dog sees you getting nervous, he'll get nervous, too. The importance of good treats cannot be underestimated in this situation. Reward your dog for staying calm in the car, being relaxed in the waiting room, and tolerating the exam. Then give your dog lots of treats and playtime once you've successfully completed the vet visit. The positive reinforcement should make the next visit go smoothly.

Puppy Classes

Within the first few months of your puppy's arrival to your household, you should start thinking about training courses. Puppies need to learn the basics of training so they can be more successful in basic adult training classes. These courses won't train your dog to be a champion in the show ring, but they will teach you and your dog how basic obedience training works. These classes are also a great way to socialize your dog with other puppies and humans.

Because Great Pyrenees are notoriously difficult to obedience train, despite their intelligence, it's important to start training practice at a young age and continue practicing throughout the dog's life. Even if you've trained past dogs, a class gives you extra incentive to show up on a weekly basis and practice in between sessions. It can be hard to keep a regular practice schedule, especially if your dog doesn't take to training well, so enrolling in training classes allows you to set aside valuable practice time with the resources you need to be successful. Once your puppy meets the age requirements of the puppy course and has his shots, start working on good training habits.

Pet Supplies to Have Ready

It's a good idea to have some basic supplies on hand before bringing your puppy home. That way, you don't have to worry about leaving your pup at home while you go shopping. Over time, you will get to know which toys and treats your dog likes the best, so focus on collecting the staples to start.

If you purchased a puppy, it might be a good idea to have a playpen or baby gate on hand. If you're concerned about your new dog having free rein of the house, it's helpful to set up barricades to prevent your pup from having accidents all over your carpet while you're not home to supervise. Just keep in mind that barricading your Great Pyrenees in a tiny confined space for long periods of time will make him go stir-crazy, especially as he grows out of his space. It's okay to keep your dog in one part of the house for short periods of time, but make sure your Great Pyrenees has plenty of room to roam throughout the day when you're able to supervise. Put food, water, your dog's crate, and/or bed in this designated space. You'll also want some sort of bedding in your dog's crate, but this doesn't have to be too fancy. You can opt to buy padding from the store, but an old blanket will also work. If you're using potty pads, make sure to have plenty on hand as your dog has accidents. Or you may want to put newspaper on the floor to make clean up easier.

Next, you'll need a good collar and leash. To start, choose a flat-buckle collar. Later on, you can decide if you want to use a harness or different training collar, but the flat collar is appropriate for most dogs. If you have an adult dog that overpowers you on walks, a harness may work better. A shelter or rescue employee can give you advice about what works best for your particular dog. While you're at the pet store, have a tag engraved with your dog's name and your contact information. Choose a sturdy 4-foot or 6-foot leash for your dog. Retractable leashes are popular, but not really appropriate for a Great Pyrenees. These leashes are comprised of a thin cord that can easily snap if your strong dog tries to chase a rabbit. Also, it's better to practice walking with your dog on your side, as opposed to leading the way or trailing behind. A sturdy leash, at least an inch wide, that you can control your dog with is a much better option. The packaging on a leash should tell you the size of dog it is meant for, so make sure the leash you buy is consistent with your dog's eventual weight.

To keep your Great Pyrenees entertained, you'll want a few toys that can stand up to your dog's jaw strength. A Great Pyrenees can tear through a stuffed animal in no time, so don't waste your time and money filling a basket with flimsy toys. Nylon, rawhide, and cow femur chews are a necessity when it comes to appeasing this dog breed. Choose a chew that will not splinter or be easily gulped down, and is large enough that your dog can't choke on it. When your dog is feeling destructive, a good chew will preserve both of your sanities!

Good toys can be expensive, but they will last longer than soft toys that will easily be destroyed. Anything made of sturdy rope or similar materials is a good option. You can buy more toys as you see what your dog prefers, but it's necessary to have a few options on hand to keep your new dog occupied.

Finally, you'll want to have a few grooming tools on hand. A pin brush and slicker brush keep the top coat shiny and tangle-free, and the undercoat from matting. A toothbrush and special dog toothpaste is helpful for keeping your Great Pyrenees's pearly whites fresh and clean. Nail clippers are essential for regular trimmings, and to take care of long claws. It's also a good idea to have gentle dog shampoo or wipes on hand for when your dog gets dirty.

Erin HOTOVY | The Complete Guide to the Great Pyrenees

How Much Will This Cost?

The initial price of getting a Great Pyrenees can be overwhelming, especially to a first-time pet owner. While you might feel like you're spending a ton of money on a dog, remember that there are a lot of one-time costs right away. While some items, like dog food and toys, will need to be purchased on a regular basis, items like nail clippers, dishes, and a leash should last the life of your pet. Of course, the price of dog supplies varies due to location and quality of supplies, but here is a rough estimate of what it will cost to take care of your Great Pyrenees in its first year.

First, let's start with the cost of the dog itself. The low end of adoption is around a hundred dollars and the high end of purchasing a dog is over a thousand. Depending on your overall budget, this could make a huge difference in whether or not a Great Pyrenees is an affordable option. Especially if you're buying a dog for showing or working purposes, prepare to spend around two thousand or more.

When it comes to purchasing the supplies listed in the previous section, you're looking at spending around $200-$400 upfront. But items like gates, kennels, and grooming supplies will last a long time, so you probably won't have to pay for these things again. Try to find supplies of moderate quality—a cheap, flimsy brush may break within a few years, forcing you to buy a new one later on. At the same time, an average pair of nail clippers will

Photo Courtesy of Danielle ODell

CHAPTER 4   Bringing Your Great Pyrenees Home

last awhile because they aren't used on a daily basis, so there's no need to buy the most expensive set in the store.

Next, you'll need to buy lots of food and treats. On average, a large bag of dog food is about $50. Depending on your Great Pyrenees's weight, you'll go through a large bag in less than a month. So, over the course of a year, you may be spending over $600 annually for food. Treats are roughly $5 a bag, and because you'll be training your Great Pyrenees often, you'll need to keep plenty on hand. In a year, it's all too easy to spend nearly a hundred dollars on training treats alone.

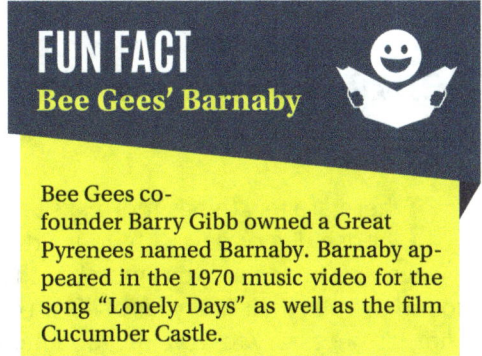

FUN FACT
Bee Gees' Barnaby

Bee Gees co-founder Barry Gibb owned a Great Pyrenees named Barnaby. Barnaby appeared in the 1970 music video for the song "Lonely Days" as well as the film Cucumber Castle.

Then you'll have to factor in veterinary visits. With any luck, your dog will be healthy and will only require a yearly checkup and vaccinations, according to his schedule. First-year vaccinations, examination, flea and tick prevention, and heartworm medication could still run you about $200. Your veterinarian may be able to recommend a health plan for your dog that will help cut down on the costs of regular medical care.

Finally, if you choose to enroll your dog in training classes, which you should, you'll find that basic group sessions cost around $75-$100 for a six-week session. In the course of the first year, you may complete one or two training courses. If you opt for private training, you'll pay even more.

So, by the end of your dog's first year in your home, it's not inconceivable to spend around $1,000-$2,000, not including the original price of your Great Pyrenees! And this is only a rough estimate of basic care. If you plan on training your dog for competitions, or they have an unexpected health issue, this number could increase dramatically. This number may seem discouraging to a new pet owner, but the money will be worth it when you have your new family member in your home. That said, the cost of taking care of a Great Pyrenees is definitely something to keep in mind before you buy or adopt. If the price of the dog is going to make it difficult to save for unexpected vet expenses, you may be better off waiting to adopt a different dog more appropriate to your needs.

CHAPTER 5
Being a Puppy Parent

There are few things more exciting than having a new puppy in your house. Every day with your little ball of fluff is different and fun. However, it's important to remember that dogs learn a lot about the world around them in their first year of life. In order to set your dog up for success in life, it's necessary to develop good habits in the early months.

Photo Courtesy of Angel Scott

CHAPTER 5   Being a Puppy Parent

Standing by Your Expectations

When you bring your dog home, it's easy to have optimistic ideas about the way your dog will behave like a perfect angel. Unfortunately, dogs like to pick up behaviors that will grate on your nerves over time. You may think that a little barking is no big deal, but you may change that stance when it's two in the morning, and your Great Pyrenees won't stop howling. Instead of correcting bad behaviors when they becomes a problem, it's easier to anticipate those behaviors and teach more acceptable ones.

> **FUN FACT**
> **Rock and Roll Pyrenees**
>
> Among his many other pets, including turkeys, peacocks, and horses, Elvis Presley had a Great Pyrenees named Muffin. The king of rock and roll had a large number of pets at Graceland, but it's rumored that he didn't care for cats.

If there are other people in your home, everyone needs to get on the same page in regards to how your dog will be allowed to behave. If you don't want to encourage your dog to beg for people food, you will likely avoid feeding your dog scraps altogether. But if your partner or kids are constantly handing off food under the table, this will undermine your efforts and make it hard for your dog to understand the household rule.

Especially with this breed, there are some behaviors that are fine for a puppy, but not for a giant dog. When correcting behaviors, keep in mind that your little guy will soon be very large. Lindsey Morrison of Golden Pond Farms recommends that you teach your puppy not to jump on people. While a little puppy won't cause much harm by jumping up to say hello, imagine the damage a 150-pound dog can do. Morrison also points out that some people don't want a large dog dominating the space of their bed or couches, so treat your puppy the same way you would treat your adult dog. If you don't want your giant Great Pyrenees hogging your bed as an adult, don't allow your little pup to snuggle under the covers. It will only make it more difficult to break these habits, as your dog will not understand the change in rules when it's fully grown.

How to Crate Train

Crates are a fantastic tool to use with your dog, and teaching your dog how to use one as a puppy is much easier than convincing him to go in the box as an adult. Crates, or kennels, can be made of plastic or wire, and provide a safe and cozy spot for your dog to hang out. They can also provide your dog with a comfortable spot to rest while you're unable to keep an eye on him, or act as restraints on car rides. It's beneficial to teach your dog that it's not scary to be in an enclosure for a short period of time.

The crate should never be used as a puppy prison. Dogs naturally love to crawl into little dens when they're stressed or scared. You may have seen dogs react to a thunderstorm by crawling under a bed or hiding under a table. A crate can provide that same level of comfort. It's also useful if a dog has a clear signal for when he's stressed out. Instead of snapping when annoyed, he can go to his crate to let people know that he needs a break. The owner should then respect this space and give the dog time to chill out. Issues arise with crates when dogs are locked inside as punishment for bad behavior, or if an owner leaves them inside for too long.

To get your puppy to explore a crate, start by placing a treat inside. Take a step back and let your dog sniff around the crate on his own. When he's ready, he'll peek inside to get the treat. Keep placing treats further back in the crate so your dog has to climb in further to reach it. Then place your dog's food and water inside and encourage him to eat meals inside. When your dog is comfortable resting in the crate, shut the gate for short periods of time and give rewards if he stays calm. Keep increasing the time spent in there until your dog can stay relaxed in the crate.

Chewing

Chewing is a behavior that all puppies do regardless of their training. This is because puppies explore the world through their mouth, and because puppies lose their puppy teeth and get adult teeth. Because you can't stop a puppy from chewing, you will have to find a way to allow them to chew that doesn't destroy your belongings or injure your dog. When you see your dog chewing on something he shouldn't, clap your hands to get their attention and say, "No chew." Then direct them to a toy or bone and offer praise if he starts to chew on it. Like with any redirection, this requires you to keep a close eye on your dog so you can notice if he starts to chew on a forbidden item.

CHAPTER 5 Being a Puppy Parent

*Photo Courtesy of
Brittany McDowell & Steven Vail*

Photo Courtesy of Jillian Olsen

CHAPTER 5   Being a Puppy Parent

As a rule, it's best to put chewable household objects out of reach. For example, if you don't want to return home to chewed slippers, keep your slippers in the closet. If your dog is persistently chewing on furniture that cannot be moved out of reach, pet stores sell sprays that are safe for dogs to eat, but which don't taste good. This may help your dog avoid gnawing on table legs. Also, try to find chew toys that your dog loves, so he will have some incentive to use them. Flavored bones are good choices.

Barking

The Great Pyrenees is one of those breeds that barks more than others. So, if you cannot handle barking in your home, this breed may not be best for you. Even if you're fine with barking and howling, it may be useful to try to cut down on excessive noise, if possible. The key is to reward your dog for being quiet. You can try connecting it to a cue word or phrase like, "Good, no bark!" if your dog fights the urge to bark at a noise he heard three blocks away. If your dog is barking too much, you can try to get his attention with a clap and redirect their behavior to something more desirable. With enough positive reinforcement, your dog might forget what he was barking about altogether.

Digging

If you allow your dog to spend time unsupervised in the yard, there's a chance he'll start digging at some point. Dogs dig because it's fun, they're hunting for underground creatures, they're trying to escape, or it's hot and they want to create a cool den. If you've worked hard on your landscaping and don't want your dog digging trenches, you'll need to watch and redirect him if he starts to dig. Get his attention and say, "No dig!" in a stern voice. When he stops and does something else, praise him.

You may notice that your dog likes to dig in the same spots. If you find yourself constantly filling the same holes, you may want to temporarily place an object in the way. This may deter your pup until he realizes he's not supposed to be doing that. Some owners will give dogs a special digging area, like a sandbox, where they're redirected to dig. This may work with the right kind of reinforcement and training, but be aware that it may backfire and make your dog think that digging is fine. Digging becomes a serious issue when he's able to burrow out from underneath the fence and escape, so if this describes your digger, you may need to reinforce your boundaries with an invisible fence or a fence that sits deeper in the ground.

Separation Anxiety

Photo Courtesy of Becca Ylitalo

Great Pyrenees are fairly sensitive dogs that are prone to separation anxiety. This negative reaction occurs when a dog is temporarily left alone. Dogs with separation anxiety will whine, scratch at the door, chew on your belongings, have accidents on the floor, and internalize serious stress. These symptoms end when you return, but will happen again the next time you leave. Because stress is not good for your dog's health, and destructive habits are not good for your home, it's important to do what you can to reduce this anxiety. If your dog freaks out when you leave, there are a few things you can try to reduce the stress.

For starters, try not to make a big deal when you come and go. Dog owners love when their pup greets them with a wagging tail, so they tend to play up that reaction by getting excited and talking in a high-pitched voice. This only teaches your dog that your return is really good, so your departure must be really bad. Instead of getting excited when you return and giving your dog hugs and kisses when you leave, try not to do anything at all. Casually walk in and out of your house and greet your dog with your normal voice and a pat on the head when he comes to greet you.

You can also reduce nervous energy by making sure your dog has his physical and mental exercise needs met. Before you leave for the day, it might help to spend some time walking or playing with your dog. When you go, leave a fun puzzle toy to keep him busy for a while, so he doesn't notice that you're not around. With any luck, this exercise will keep him chill enough to sleep for a little while until you come home.

If all else fails, talk to a vet about finding ways to help your dog calm down. They may recommend medication, supplements, or other home remedies.

Running Away

"Pyrenees also like to determine their own boundaries. If not well contained they may roam a large distance from your home, creating their own circular perimeter which they will guard fiercely. However that circle may well include roads streets and other people's property and pets. A good fence and regular training of the dog teaching her where the boundaries are and what she is guarding will go a long way to preventing this behavior."

Susan Grimm
Grimm Acres, Diversified

Like his ancestors who roamed the open mountain range, your Great Pyrenees will want to roam wherever he pleases. Unfortunately, dogs can get lost or hurt without supervision from their humans, so it's best if they stay contained in your home, or go out on a leash. Your Great Pyrenees is intelligent and makes his own rules. If your door or gate is slightly ajar, your dog will squeeze through the gap. If your fence is too low or there are gaps, your dog will find a way out. If you think you can trust your dog to hang out in the front yard while you rake leaves, expect your dog to bolt when your back is turned. Having your dog run off is terrifying, so it's important to put some precautions in place to prevent this from happening.

First, make sure your home is airtight. Check your doors and fences so your dog can't escape. Let all of your family members know about your dog's propensity to wander so they are extra vigilant. Always keep a collar with identification on your dog so if he does get loose, he can be identified and returned. Always walk your dog on a sturdy leash.

There are some behavioral tricks that may reduce the risk of your dog running away. Teach your dog to wait for you to go through a door before he goes through. This will keep him from squeezing through gaps to get outside. Also, work on your "come" command from the very start of your dog's life. If your dog gets out, with this command in place, you may be able to get him to return to you.

Bedtime

Photo Courtesy of Jenni Fellman

Dogs do well with routines, so following the same schedule can help with your dog's good behavior. If you go to bed at the same time every night, your dog will sync with your schedule and settle down around that time, too. Take your dog out to use the bathroom the last thing you do before bed. This will keep him from needing to go once you've settled down, and give him the cue that he needs to settle down, too.

If your dog is crate trained, this is a great place to have him sleep. Not only is it comfy and cozy, but you can keep him contained during the night so he doesn't wander around the house and get in trouble. If it helps your puppy feel more secure, you can even place his crate in your bedroom. That way, he will know that he hasn't been abandoned. As your dog gets older, he will be more comfortable with longer periods without interaction from you, especially as his bladder grows and he no longer needs to pee on an hourly basis.

Leaving Your Dog Home Alone

Adult Great Pyrenees do fine if left alone for a workday. It's best if they get exercise and attention before and after you get home (and at lunchtime) but you generally don't have to worry about them destroying your home. Puppies are a different story. They have tons of energy, don't know the rules of the house yet, and want to chew, climb, and pee on everything. They're also not used to being alone for several hours at a time, and this may freak them out. To get through the puppy stage, there are a few things you can do to keep your puppy happy and your home in one piece.

CHAPTER 5 Being a Puppy Parent

Some owners like to put their dog in a doggy day care. They can drop their dog off when they go to work and pick him up on the way home, knowing that his needs were met during the day. Day cares can be expensive, but it's worth it if your dog doesn't do well alone and your schedule doesn't allow you to take time to check in with your pup throughout the day. Another option is to hire a dog walker or sitter. This way, your dog gets exercise, human interaction, and a chance to relieve himself. Some people even offer daily pet sitting services in their home. If you need someone to watch your dog for a little while, there are tons of apps, like Rover and Wag, and other resources out there for finding temporary help.

Puppies are precious, but they require a lot of time and energy to teach how to live in a human's home. It is the owner's job to teach them how to behave properly and redirect undesirable behavior. It's a hard job and there's no shame in getting some extra help! Vets, trainers, breeders, and pet sitters are all fantastic resources to turn to if you're worried you're not giving your puppy what he needs. Your dog learns so much in the first year of his life, so plan to teach your dog good behaviors early, and break bad behaviors before they become habits.

CHAPTER 6
Housetraining

If you've adopted an adult dog, you probably don't have to worry about housetraining him. Think of all the accidents you don't have to clean up! If you bought a little puppy, however, you've got your work cut out for you. Housetraining takes some patience, attention, and a willingness to clean stinky messes. The Great Pyrenees is intelligent, but can be stubborn, so make sure potty training is positive, and your dog will learn in no time!

Different Options for Housetraining

HELPFUL TIP
Yard Cleanup

Dogs appreciate a clean, waste-free outdoor space as much as their humans. Residential yard-cleaning services are available in most areas for busy pet owners who lack the time or ability to clean up after their dogs in their backyards. Check your local listings for dog waste clean-up services in your area and see if such services might be a good fit for your lifestyle.

The Great Pyrenees is not an apartment dweller, so you don't have to worry about grass replacement devices made for dogs to use the bathroom inside. You wouldn't want to anyway, seeing as your big dog can produce big messes! You'll want to teach your dog to go outside from the start. This will help your dog connect a certain place in your backyard with performing bodily functions.

However, puppies need to go much more often than adult dogs, and humans can't always be there to make sure they get outside in time. If you're having trouble with accidents in your house, you may choose to buy puppy pads and put them wherever your dog spends the bulk of his time. These absorbent pads contain scents that prompt your dog to go to the bathroom. So, if your dog is going to potty inside, he will more likely choose the pad than the floor. These may be useful in the early days, but should slowly be moved away from as your dog gets older. It can be tempting to buy different mats and pads to avoid having to take your dog out frequently, but with a Great Pyrenees, you'll want to always make the outdoors your first choice.

CHAPTER 6 Housetraining

Photo Courtesy of Becca Ylitalo

Getting into a Routine

It takes a while to get the timing figured out, but before long, you'll find patterns between the time your dog eats and drinks and when they need to go out. Every dog is different, so observing your dog and watching for cues is important. Many dogs will start to sniff around their space or "assume the position" when they feel the urge, giving you just enough time to distract them and get them to their outdoor spot.

It's also good to remember that puppies have much smaller bladders than adult dogs. As they age, they can go a little longer without having to relieve themselves. If you're bringing home a new puppy, take your dog outside every half hour to hour. Even if he doesn't potty, he will have the opportunity to try. As your puppy gets older, these trips will be less frequent. By the time your dog is a year old, he'll be able to hold it for hours. Starting out, it may be helpful to set a repeating alarm for every thirty minutes to an hour, so you don't forget to let the dog out.

On your trips outside, try to go to the same part of your yard every time. Dog waste contains special smells that tell your dog that this is a good place to go to the bathroom. Taking your dog to the same spot is a way of telling him what he's supposed to do. When your dog is finished, give them lots of praise. Even if you're in an enclosed yard, keep your dog on a leash so you can guide him to the potty area, and he won't get distracted and want to play. Teach your dog that there is a time for business and a time for play, and he'll be less likely to wander around your backyard with no clue what to do.

Rewarding Positive Behavior

Photo Courtesy of Marisa Alford

Positive reinforcement is a powerful tool for Great Pyrenees. They're sensitive, so they want to make their human happy, but they also want to do what makes them happy. You can combine these two motivators by giving your dog tons of love and lots of treats when he successfully goes potty outside. Every time your dog does what you want, he should receive some type of reward. This tells him that he's doing a good job, and will shape his behavior.

Avoid punishment or fear tactics at all costs. These will upset a dog and can lead to even worse behaviors, like having accidents in the house, but in hidden places. Many owners make the mistake of yelling at their dog when they find a pet mess, which could have occurred hours previous. Dogs do not have a memory that effectively connects past occurrences to present consequences. If you rub a dog's nose in a mess, he's going to be confused and upset. He won't understand that the poop on your floor has anything to do with something he did wrong. However, he will know that you're confusingly upset with him, and that makes learning and positive reinforcement more difficult.

Every time you successfully get your dog outside to potty and he receives a reward, you create a learning moment. If your dog has an accident, you've essentially lost a learning moment. The only thing you can do is clean up the mess really well and remove those scents that could cause your dog to become a repeat offender. Then keep an eye on your dog and try again next time.

CHAPTER 6 Housetraining

Crate Training for Housetraining Use

"Some potty train instantly and some take a bit longer. I believe in crate training and I recommend getting the biggest crate you can for training. I like to have mine ready with a comfy bed and an area for food and water. Try to have a routine, when possible, for feeding and taking them out right after meal times. I like to train mine to go to the bathroom on the edge of the property so they do not poop right by the back door. If you walk them in the beginning, even if you have a fenced yard, and show them where you want them to go, they typically catch on quickly. Giving treats whenever they go outside and where you want may help a lot."

Lindsey Morrison
Golden Pond Farms

Crate training can be extremely useful for housetraining because dogs generally don't like to soil their den. A crate should be large enough for your dog to turn around, but not so large that he can comfortably create a potty corner. For this breed, you'll want to buy a puppy crate and an adult crate. A puppy with lots of room to roam will eliminate when he feels the urge to go, but a dog in a crate will want to hold it until he has more space. So, if your dog is comfortable in a crate, let him hang out there for an hour while you complete your household tasks. When that time is up, take him directly from the crate to the yard and reward him when he goes to the bathroom. This will

Photo Courtesy of Megan Wallace

help reduce your dog's confusion about where is acceptable and not acceptable to go potty.

    The crate will also help your dog to understand that he will not have as many opportunities to go out at night and that he needs to get your attention when it's an emergency. When you crate your dog at night, you will be able to hear his cries that tell you he needs to go. When you hear it, put him on a leash and take him to his potty spot. When he's finished, bring him right back in and place him in the crate. Avoid too much interaction or activity so your dog doesn't incorrectly assume it's playtime. Not only will crate use at night keep your house clean, but it will help you increase your teachable moments.

Photo Courtesy of Shelly Bergeson

CHAPTER 6 Housetraining

Playpens and Doggy Doors

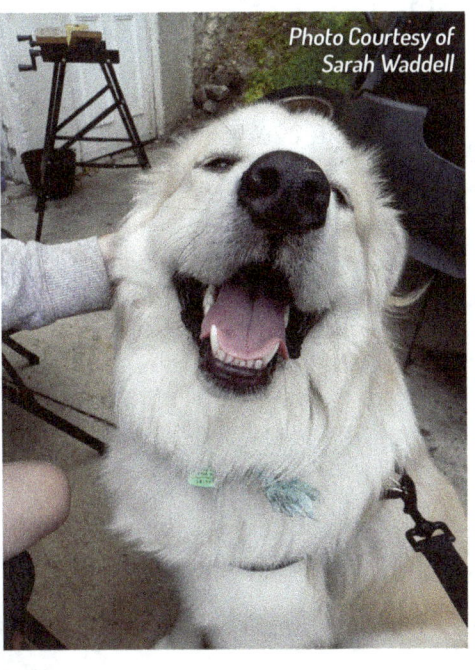

Photo Courtesy of Sarah Waddell

Many owners like to set up a confined space for their puppy to keep accidents in one easy-to-clean spot. A gate or playpen can allow your puppy to move around, while keeping him off carpet and near newspaper or puppy pads. If the space is small enough, it may work similarly to the crate, and the dog will not want to go potty in his den. If you know that there will be times when you can't keep a close eye on your dog, this may be a good temporary set-up for your home.

Once the dog understands that his bathroom is outside, a doggy door may make it easier for your dog to take care of his needs without needing a human to let him out. This may be a good option if your Great Pyrenees is generally well-behaved and can be trusted to come and go as he pleases. This makes life more convenient for owners, as they don't have to worry if they won't make it home in time to let their dog out, or worry about their dog getting stuck in the rain. However, keep in mind that having a hole in your door is not always ideal. If a dog can come and go, that means other small creatures can do the same. And, if your dog is a skilled hunter, he can easily bring you his trophies. A doggy door can be useful under the right circumstances, but think about the security of your home before you put one in your door.

Housetraining doesn't have to be a pain, but it's understandable if you find yourself getting frustrated at the accidents. Do your best to avoid getting annoyed at your dog because he will feed off the negative emotions. Instead, keep your cool when you clean up messes and give your dog tons of praise and love for getting it right. Positive training is powerful for this breed, so make sure you give your dog tons of tries to use the bathroom outside, and reward every successful attempt. In no time, you'll forget that you ever had to worry about your dog using your home as a toilet.

CHAPTER 7
Socializing with People and Animals

If you're new to owning a dog, it's easy to get so caught up in housetraining and obedience training that you forget how to teach your dog to interact with others. This type of training is just as important as, if not more important than, obedience training if you plan on ever taking your dog where other people or dogs are present. Even if you live alone and rarely take your dog out, something as simple as going to the vet can be made much easier by teaching your dog socialization skills. Dogs get the most out of socialization between four and eight months old, so don't wait when it comes to exposing your pup to new experiences. Good socialization practice as a pup will set your dog up to have a successful adulthood.

Photo Courtesy of Jillian Olsen

CHAPTER 7   Socializing with People and Animals

Importance of Good Socialization

A socialized dog is a pleasure to be around, because he is calm and friendly toward others. A dog that is fearful of other people and dogs is difficult to take places. Imagine taking your dog to the dog park on a nice day. You want your energetic dog to get plenty of exercise so he will be calm and content for the rest of the day. A dog that is used to being around other dogs will run, play, and have a good time. A dog that does not feel comfortable around others will cower, growl, or run back to the gate and wait for you to take him home.

Dogs need to feel comfortable around other people, too. If you have people over to your house, or take your dog to the farmer's market with you, you don't want your dog to avoid friendly interactions, growl, or nip at people who want to say hi. Part of the fun of having a dog is to share the joy your dog brings with others. If you can't leave the house or have visitors without upsetting your dog, this can make dog ownership difficult.

You never want your dog to be scared. Stress is not good for your dog's health, and dogs often react to fear by lashing out. The last thing you want is for your dog to hurt another dog or human because he felt unsafe. For this reason, it's imperative that you spend time socializing your dog. Luckily, this can be a lot of fun! Socialization skills can be gained through positive experiences. Take your pup to the park or have a drink at a patio and let strangers give your dog treats. Or, let your friends come over and play fetch with your dog—or have them bring their dogs for a puppy party! There are lots of things you can do to expose your dog to interactions with humans and dogs—just remember to keep it positive.

Behavior Around Other Dogs

"Making good choices is important, socialize too early and you risk getting your Pyr sick. Wait until your puppy is totally covered by his vaccinations. Don't allow larger dogs to put their weight on your puppy or play to rough. Otherwise your puppy could get injured."

Sharon Reile
Schnee Bar of the Great Plains

Great Pyrenees are generally good with other dogs, so you should feel comfortable having your dog interact with others of his kind. However, not all dogs are super playful with others. This can be a result of breeding or prior negative experiences. You'll even see differences in littermates when it comes to how social they are. Some dogs are more dominant and some are more passive, and that's perfectly normal. What's not normal is when a dog is aggressive or fearful around others.

When two dogs meet, they will sniff each other. While it seems weird for a dog to sniff another dog's behind, there is nothing improper about

Photo Courtesy of
Gilbert and Danielle Crawford
Double Dewclaw Ranch

this interaction. Never discourage your dog from sniffing a rump because this is how your dog learns about other dogs. Dogs can sniff out the sex of another dog, amongst other bits of information that scientists haven't completely figured out. So, when your dog sniffs another, it's the canine equivalent to humans shaking hands.

Watch your dog's body language, because nonverbal cues say a lot about what he's thinking. A wagging tail and a "bow" is an invitation to play. Gentle play biting around the face and neck is considered safe roughhousing. Dogs also love to chase each other, which is great exercise.

> **FUN FACT**
> **Big Screen Pets**
>
> Great Pyrenees dogs have appeared in a number of television shows as well as movies. One of the earliest on-screen performance for one of these dogs was in the 1932 film *Horse Feathers,* where a Great Pyrenees is seen in the dog catcher's wagon. Other notable films starring Great Pyrenees are *Dumb and Dumber, Finding Neverland,* and *Santa Buddies.*

You don't want a dog that's cowering with his tail between his legs. This means that your dog feels nervous. A dog may show submission by rolling over. This isn't necessarily a sign that your dog is afraid, but is meant to show other dogs that he doesn't want to challenge them. Growling, baring teeth, or hair standing up on their shoulders means a dog is upset and will fight back if necessary.

To encourage positive encounters with other dogs, you'll want to start slow and control the interactions. Start by having a friendly dog over for a play date and let your puppy learn from their elder. If your dog feels comfortable around a few canine friends, you may try to take him to the park and see how he does with strangers. A trip to the pet store may also be helpful for meeting new dogs. Of course, training classes are highly beneficial for socialization because they require your dog to be in an enclosed space with other pups, but in a more controlled environment.

While you can't always control other dogs, you can control your own behavior. Try to stay relaxed so your dog knows that there's nothing to fear. Speak to your dog in a calm voice and bring treats with you so your dog connects the experience with rewards. Give your dog some space to interact and avoid hovering. Your dog will notice if you're standing guard and wonder if he is in danger. If you want your dog to be relaxed, you have to lead by example.

Properly Greeting New People

Great Pyrenees are friendly around familiar people, but they may be cautious around strangers. Because they were first bred to protect, you may find that their reactions to strangers may be interpreted as unfriendly. To socialize your dog, you need to teach him that friendly strangers do not need to raise alarm.

When starting out, try not to overwhelm your dog with too many people. Have some friends over and let them give your dog treats and play with him. When your dog can be friendly around people you know, introduce him to people you don't know. Go on a walk and ask a passerby to give your dog a treat and give him a pet. If you like to go to outdoor bars or restaurants, you'll hardly have to ask someone to approach your pup. If you want someone to win over your dog, have them offer a tasty treat. As your dog becomes more comfortable around people, start taking him to busier places where there are more sights, sounds, and sniffs.

It's also important to introduce your pup to all sorts of people. For example, if your dog is only used to interacting with women, a man will be noticeably different and could set off the "stranger danger" alert. Or, if your dog is used to interacting with short people, a very tall person may startle him. Letting your dog hang out with a diverse crowd of people will make him feel more at ease around strangers because he's already had a positive experience with people who look different.

Photo Courtesy of
Callie Littlefield

CHAPTER 7   Socializing with People and Animals

Great Pyrenees and Children

This breed is fairly good with kids and may even feel protective of them. However, all dogs need to be supervised when meeting children. Children, like dogs, can be unpredictable, and don't always act how adults would like. Not only do you need to teach your dog to be gentle around young children, but you need to teach young children to be gentle with your pup.

Photo Courtesy of Michelle Hiner

Start by instructing children how to properly pet a dog. To be safe, have them stick to the dog's back so they avoid the eyes, nose, mouth, ears, and tail. Long, soft strokes down the dog's back are best and will help your dog feel more relaxed, too. Tell the kids to remain calm around the dog so your dog won't get too wound up and accidentally injure someone. Your little puppy probably won't do too much damage to anyone, but a large adult dog can easily knock a child over if they play too roughly. A lot of noise and action can frighten a dog. If the children can't calm down, the dog needs to be able to escape and hang out in his safe space. Never force a dog to spend time with anyone he doesn't want to be near (except the vet). If a dog feels threatened or has been hurt by rough play, he will snap, which may injure a child and make them averse to dogs in the future. So, if you want your pup to grow up alongside kids, make sure everyone is happy and safe.

Socialization skills are critical in the first year of your dog's life. If your dog doesn't get out into the world until adulthood, he will have a harder time becoming accustomed to interacting with dogs and humans. Good socialization skills will make your dog happier because he can enjoy the company of others without getting scared, and it will make you happier because you'll be able to take your dog anywhere!

CHAPTER 8
Great Pyrenees and Your Other Pets

"Their normal nature is to be with other animals and they are very patient and passive on average. Some can be food aggressive so it is important to work with them from day one. I have had more problems with other dogs dominating or being too aggressive/rough with my Pyrs than the other way around. But typically they are so patient until they are pushed too far; when that line is crossed they have no problem putting another dog/animal in their place."

Lindsey Morrison
Golden Pond Farms

Photo Courtesy of Amber M Lecy

CHAPTER 8 Great Pyrenees and Your Other Pets

Perhaps you're not new to dog ownership, but this is your first Great Pyrenees. Great Pyrenees will get along just fine with your other pets, as long as you practice good socialization skills from the start. Because we don't always understand what our dogs are thinking, it's important to set them up for success so you aren't blindsided by bad behavior. This chapter will help you better understand the ins and outs of adding another pup to the pack.

Introducing Your New Puppy to Other Pets

When it comes to introducing your new pup to your other pets, it's best to slowly integrate your dog into the group. If you suddenly bring a new dog into your home, your other pets may be caught off guard. If your existing pets are dog-friendly, then they probably won't have a lot of trouble accepting their new friend. But, if your other pets aren't sure what to think about a new doggy sibling, they may react negatively. If you can slowly allow your pets to get to know one another, then you'll be likely to have more success.

If possible, try to have your puppy meet his new family before he's officially released into your care. Talk to your breeder about arranging a meet-up. Your breeder will give you advice and help you find the best way for your dogs to meet your new puppy. Be sure to ask before bringing your dogs over—breeders are understandably concerned about the health and well-being of their pups. If you're adopting, talk to your shelter about setting up a meeting with your new dog and your other pets. They may allow you to take the dog home for a short trial, just to be sure everyone gets along.

Neutral meeting spots are ideal for the first meeting because no dog will feel territorial over their space. Your existing dogs may be friendly, but they may not like a little puppy coming into their space and messing up their smells or playing with their toys. It's hard to know if your dog will be territorial until another dog challenges their space. For this reason, a park or a friend's home is a good choice for this first meeting, as neither dog will have a connection to the space.

After that, a meeting in your home will help your new dog acclimate to their new house, plus help your older dog accept the fact that they're going to have to share with another dog. Regardless of your location, make sure the dogs have plenty of space and are not forced to interact in close quarters. If your dogs don't want to play, don't push it. When they're comfortable, they'll naturally begin to interact.

Photo Courtesy of Becca Ylitalo

CHAPTER 8 Great Pyrenees and Your Other Pets

Cats are a different story, especially because Great Pyrenees have a moderate prey drive. You definitely don't need to push a cat into a small space with your dog. In fact, you should give your cat plenty of opportunities to stay out of your pup's reach. While some cats become best friends with dogs, others want nothing to do with canines, and are perfectly content to keep their distance. A cat tree is a necessity in a home with dogs. That way, if your cat feels threatened, it can jump out of reach, instead of having to resort to using claws. Your Great Pyrenees will probably want to sniff the cat and figure out what that furry creature is, but make sure your dog doesn't play too roughly. If you have a new puppy, you may be able to teach him to be gentle around cats, so their instinct is suppressed. With an adult dog, it could be harder to teach him not to bother the cat when he desperately wants to chase it.

Pack Mentality

Dog owners and breeders have different ideas about how pack mentality plays into your dogs' relationships with one another. Some believe that canines follow certain rules of order within a group while others believe that our dogs of today are so removed from their ancestors that pack behavior doesn't affect our domesticated breeds. Whether or not you ascribe to the ideas about pack influence, it's helpful to know how dogs see social order.

Some dogs are dominant while other dogs are submissive. This doesn't mean that your dog is either aggressive or afraid, but some dogs just naturally yield to others. If you have multiple dogs in your home, you may find that one is a leader and the other is a follower. This is completely normal behavior. If your existing dog is an adult, you may notice your older dog displaying some signals to your puppy that appear unfriendly. Puppies are notorious for being pests, so your older dog may just be putting him in his place. Puppies tend to shape up and calm down when an older dog growls or barks. As long as no one is agitated for a prolonged amount of time or gets hurt, then it's normal to see this type of behavior as your puppy learns how to act around other dogs.

When it comes to training your dogs to behave in your home, try acting as the pack leader. Some trainers think that dogs will learn to respect their owner's rules if they take control of the pack. While it would be silly to growl at your dog to establish dominance, there are some things you might want to try to establish order. Instead of giving your dogs their meal before you sit down to eat, wait to feed your dogs until you're done with your meal. The submissive dog in the pack usually waits for the leader to eat,

so you're showing your dogs that you're the alpha. When you go through a doorway with your dog, have him wait for you to pass through, then invite him to follow. Not only are you showing your dog that you're in charge, but it's a good habit to practice so your Great Pyrenees doesn't rush outside whenever he gets a chance. You may not believe in treating your dogs like their ancient ancestors, but it's never a bad idea to practice good manners with your pups.

Fighting and Bad Behavior

The biggest concern you'll face when bringing a new dog into a home with other established dogs is the potential for fighting. It can be hard to understand what causes dogs to get irritated with one another. As humans, we don't always see the signs before a fight breaks out. Something as seemingly innocuous as eye contact can send a dog into fight mode. Then, when a fight breaks out, you have to worry about how you're going to break it up without getting hurt. One thing you can do to prevent fights is watch your dogs' body language and know when to defuse the situation.

As stated earlier, dogs send a lot of information about how they're feeling though nonverbal cues. Fur standing on end, bared teeth, and raised shoulders tell you that a dog is ready to strike. Growling is your final warning that your dog is upset before they act out. If you see any of these signs, find a way to safely separate the dogs. Clap your hands or make a loud noise to distract both dogs. If this doesn't work, call one dog to go outside. Some space will help them cool down and forget what they were squabbling about. Avoid grabbing your angry dog because he may not realize that his human is trying to help the situation and could turn around and bite.

If your dogs begin to fight before you can distract them, make a loud noise to break their focus. Some owners like to use a can filled with rocks because it's loud enough to slightly startle. If this doesn't work, try to place a physical barrier between the dogs without getting too close. A baking sheet or chair may be enough to break them apart. If you need to physically separate two dogs, again, never reach for a collar. Your hand will be too close to a mouth, and a dog's teeth can do a lot of damage to a person. Instead, try grabbing one dog's hind legs and slowly pull him backward until he is out of reach of the other dog. If it's safe, clip a leash on the dog and place him in another room, or send him outside. Then give your dogs a little time and space to cool off and only allow them to be in the same room once they've relaxed.

Raising Littermates

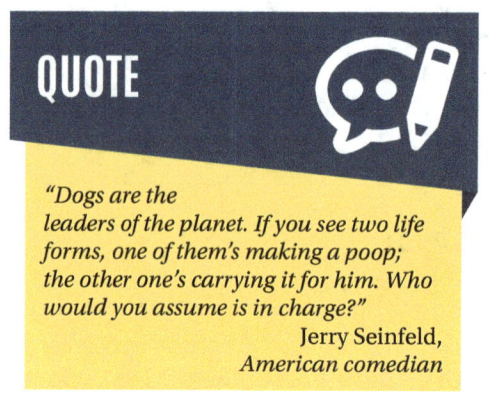

"Dogs are the leaders of the planet. If you see two life forms, one of them's making a poop; the other one's carrying it for him. Who would you assume is in charge?"

Jerry Seinfeld,
American comedian

Some people are so enamored with the idea of buying a Great Pyrenees that they want to double the fun with two puppies. While it's fun to have multiple dogs in the house, be aware that littermates can pose their own challenges to owners. For some reason, littermates often suffer from "littermate syndrome," which is a term used to describe bad behavior exhibited by puppies from the same litter. Sometimes littermates are so distracted by each other that they don't listen to their owner. Some trainers won't take littermates in their group classes because of how difficult it is to get the dogs to focus. Great Pyrenees can be difficult to train in the first place, so having two that cannot focus on the task at hand while their sibling is around can add stress.

Littermates can also experience a form of separation anxiety if one is separated from the other. For example, if you need to take one dog to the vet and not the other, both dogs will get upset, making them hard to handle. You may not have to separate the dogs often, but when you do, you'll have a harder time controlling either dog.

If you want two dogs, it might be a good idea to buy them at separate times. That way, you can work on raising one puppy before adding another to your home. You'll have fewer upfront costs and get a little practice raising one Great Pyrenees. Then you can use everything you learned to make raising a second dog easier. Or, if you want two puppies within a short timeframe, see if you can get them from separate litters. That way, you won't have to deal with the strange behaviors that can arise from raising two littermates together.

If you do purchase littermates, try to find ways to keep the two pups apart early on in their lives. Take one pup on a walk while your partner or friend walks the other one. When you have to run to the store, leave one at home with your family members while the other rides in your car. That way, they'll be able to cope when they have to be apart.

What if My Pets Don't Get Along?

When you bring your new puppy home, you want to be able to add to your happy furry family. It can be a lot of fun to have multiple pets under one roof. However, our pets don't always get along. You can try a few techniques to slowly acquaint your pets, watch for nonverbal cues, and even get trainers involved, but not all animals will get along. Certain breeds (and species) aren't always dog-friendly, even if your pup is sweet as can be. Past negative experiences and poor socialization can also make a dog hesitant to be close to other dogs. If you've tried everything and your pets don't get along to the extent that you worry for their safety, it's time to make some tough decisions.

Photo Courtesy of Rebecca M. Robida

Talk about your options with a trainer who specializes in dog behaviors, a vet, or your breeder. They may be able to diagnose a problem that you haven't noticed. But, if your pets are in danger because of fighting, it may be best to return your pup to the breeder, or find a new home for a pet. It's a hard decision to make, but in the end, you don't want one of your animals to become seriously injured while in your care. There is nothing more important than the safety of your pets, so make them a priority, even if you've been dreaming of a home with lots of furry friends.

Having multiple pets is a joy! It can be a lot of fun to watch your animals form their own pack, with you as the leader. A good relationship doesn't always happen overnight, so give your dogs plenty of time to get to know each other. Especially in the early days, keep a close eye on your dogs so you're ready to break up any potential fight in an instant. And, if you've tried your best and you worry that your pets aren't safe together, talk to your breeder about returning your puppy, or find the best possible home for a pet. At the end of the day, your pets' safety and happiness is the most important thing.

CHAPTER 9
Physical and Mental Exercise

Exercise is vital for your dog's physical and mental well-being. Any dog owner can confirm that a tired dog is a good dog. When dogs have too much energy, they tend to get themselves in trouble because they create their own games to keep themselves entertained. Plus, exercise helps your dog stay at a healthy weight and keeps his muscles strong to support his skeletal system. Your Great Pyrenees needs about an hour of exercise a day. However, this doesn't mean that you have to regularly take your dog on an hour-long walk to fulfill these needs. There are lots of different ways to give your dog exercise throughout the day that can be a lot of fun for both of you.

Photo Courtesy of Allissa Brulla

CHAPTER 9 Physical and Mental Exercise

Exercise Requirements

Photo Courtesy of Kasey Proulx

The average Great Pyrenees needs about an hour's worth of exercise a day. Even so, exercise requirements vary from dog to dog, so as yours matures, you'll be able to determine the sweet spot between pent-up energy and complete exhaustion. You should schedule time for exercise throughout the day so your dog can alternate between activity and rest. The early morning is a good time for your dog to stretch his legs. When you take him out for his bathroom break, give yourself some extra time to walk around the block. It doesn't have to be a long walk, but if your dog has some time to walk around in the morning, he'll be more likely to behave himself for the rest of the morning because he's not immediately desperate for entertainment.

If your dog suffers from separation anxiety, this morning exercise is particularly important. A tired dog will be able to settle down when you leave the house in the morning for work. If your dog has too much energy early in the day, you may want to make time for a longer walk or even a short run. Or, while you get ready for the day, you can toss a ball. That way, by the time you leave the house, your dog will be ready for a nap.

Some afternoon activity will also keep your dog from getting too bored. This can simply involve tossing a ball to your dog for a few minutes during a lunch break to and keep him from being a couch potato. Because some owners are unable to come home during the middle of the day, dog walkers are a great resource for getting your dog outside. These days, hiring a dog walker is as simple as using an app to connect with a trusted individual to take your pup on a quick walk.

For convenience's sake, many dog owners do the bulk of their exercising in the evening. However, if you live in a warm climate, it might be better for your furry friend to spend time outside earlier in the day. When it's hot and sunny, the sidewalks can get so hot that a dog's paws get burned. As a rule of thumb, if it's so hot it's uncomfortable for you to walk around in bare feet, it's too hot to walk your dog without protective footwear. With Great Pyrenees in particular, you'll want to be mindful of the temperature during your time outside. While these dogs do great in the cold, they don't love hot weather.

If a long walk isn't possible, a trip to the dog park or playing games in the backyard can burn off some energy before bedtime. When you're ready to settle down at night, you don't want your dog to be running laps around you, begging for attention. Keep your walks short and bring water along. Also make air conditioning readily available when your dog is ready to come inside. Heat-related illnesses are more likely to occur in this breed, so be careful not to push your dog too far when it's warm outside.

Photo Courtesy of Michelle Hiner

CHAPTER 9   Physical and Mental Exercise

Different Types of Exercise to Try

Exercise doesn't have to be a drag. Many times, new dog owners have all of the best intentions of going on daily walks. But, when other things come up and the weather isn't ideal, it's hard to make sure your dog consistently gets his daily exercise. Rather than walking the same route day after day, try to mix up your daily activities. You never know what your dog will be into until you try it. As you get to know your dog, keep introducing new activities and skills into his repertoire. If you're a runner, however, you'll have to go solo. These dogs will not want to run for long (unless they are chasing a predator) and are certainly not distance runners. Take your Great Pyrenees for an out-and-back, and you'll find yourself dragging your tired pooch all the way home.

> **FUN FACT**
> **Duke the Dog**
>
> In 2014, a Great Pyrenees named Duke was elected honorary mayor of Cormorant, a small Minnesota village. The election was a fundraiser for the town, where each vote cost a dollar. Duke served as mayor for several years and passed away on February 21, 2019, at the age of 13.

If you live in a mountainous area with a comfortable climate, try taking your Great Pyrenees on a hike. This dog was originally bred to roam the mountainside, so he'll have a great time climbing up and down rocks.

If you're an avid skier, you might want to try skijoring. This is a fancy name for skiing while being pulled by your dog. Great Pyrenees are perfect for this sport because they are strong, energetic, and love the snow. This activity is easier if your dog knows some basic commands. Even if your dog isn't a whiz at obedience training, you may find that he really takes to the sport and is motivated to learn. You may need to buy some special equipment, but once you have the supplies you need, you'll just need a wide, snowy area to practice. Taking your dog for a walk in the deep snow is not a lot of fun, but skiing with your dog can be very exciting.

If you're looking for a way to beat the summer heat without going stir-crazy inside, you may want to try to take your Great Pyrenees swimming. A love for water isn't necessarily a genetic trait in these dogs, but some Great Pyrenees love to paddle around on a warm day. When taking your dog out for their first swim, stay close and keep an eye on him as some dogs are not natural swimmers and may struggle. If your dog likes getting wet but isn't a strong swimmer, you can buy a doggy lifejacket from your local pet store to keep your pooch safe in the water. If your older Great Pyrenees has joint issues as he ages, swimming is a great low-impact exercise for delicate, achy joints.

Not all Great Pyrenees are crazy about playing fetch, but you may have some success with your pooch, especially if you introduce the game early on. A game of fetch teaches your dog how to retrieve an item and drop it at your feet. Some breeds are natural fetchers, but the Great Pyrenees isn't always interested in playing by human rules. But, if you can get your dog to chase an object, he'll have a lot of fun bounding around the yard.

Photo Courtesy of Emily Sharon Thompson

CHAPTER 9   Physical and Mental Exercise

Tug-of-war may also be a fun game. Buy a sturdy tug toy meant for large breeds and give one end to your dog. At first, give gentle tugs to show your dog what to do. Eventually, he'll figure it out and want to play. Don't be afraid to give your dog a strong tug, as this large breed can hold its own. When you pull on the rope, you can wiggle it from side to side, but avoid lateral movements, as dogs' necks aren't meant to be jerked up and down. If your dog gets too aggressive with this game, stop and refuse to play until he's willing to play by your rules.

There is no shortage of fun things to do to keep your dog's heart pumping and muscles working. To keep things fresh, try to rotate a variety of exercises. Otherwise, you and your dog may get bored with the same old walk and be less likely to go out at all. This breed doesn't need a ton of strenuous exercise, but it does need fresh air and a way to burn energy.

Mental Exercise

When dog owners think about giving their dogs exercise, they tend to think about long walks or running around the dog park. However, mental exercise is just as important when it comes to your dog's overall health and well-being. When dogs get bored, they entertain themselves by being naughty. Or, they get anxious.

The good news is that there are a lot of physical activities that get your dog to use his brain. Fetch and tug both require some strategy, so your dog's mind will be active as his body works hard to win the game. Even going on a walk exposes him to a lot of sights, sounds, and smells, so your dog will actively take in all of the information around you.

Some dogs go crazy for puzzle toys. These are toys that require your dog to do a little work to get food or a treat. Some make your dog slide a compartment open or pull a little drawer to get a treat. Others are balls filled with dog food that your dog has to maneuver in the right way to get the pieces of food to fall out. Others are like a rubber ball with a treat inside that needs to be bounced in just the right way to release the food. All of these are a ton of fun and keep your dog active when other forms of play are not possible. Try a few popular toys before you buy a whole bunch of puzzles, so you pick the ones your dog likes best. If you fill these toys with your dog's favorite food, even the most stubborn dog will work to get the treat out.

Chewing is an entertaining activity for dogs. There are many different chew toys on the market, so it may take some trial and error to find one

Photo Courtesy of Rachel Rains

your dog loves the most. If your pup isn't a big chewer, you may want to try flavored bones that keep your dog interested. When choosing a chew, pick a large one that your Great Pyrenees can't gobble down in one sitting. Also, make sure the chew doesn't have any small pieces that can become detached, or sharp splinters. It's best to supervise your dog the first few times he tries the chew object, just to make sure it's safe. Then, once you feel confident that your dog can chew without choking or getting hurt, you can give it to your dog when you need a little peace and quiet, or when you have to leave the house for a while.

Great Pyrenees have a lot of energy, but you have to be careful. Too much high-impact exercise over a long period of time may be hard on his joints, and exercising in warm weather can make your dog ill. This breed can be stubborn at times, so it's important not to get frustrated if your dog doesn't go along with your dreams of being a world-class Frisbee team. Find activities that the two of you love to do together, and exercise won't have to feel like a chore.

CHAPTER 10
Training Your Great Pyrenees

"Great Pyrenees are independent thinkers and can be quite stubborn. Consistency is very important. They are not for everyone. If you are expecting a dog like a German Shepherd or Rottweiler then this dog is not for you. Be prepared to make time to take him /her to training classes."

Susie Wong
Darlington Great Pyrenees

CHAPTER 10 Training Your Great Pyrenees

Obedience training is an important part of dog ownership that is frequently overlooked by owners. Without the right knowledge and support, training can be a struggle, and owners often give up when their dog isn't responding. This breed can be particularly hard to train because these dogs can be stubborn. But this makes regular training all the more necessary. Great Pyrenees are giant dogs that can cause trouble if they misbehave. Plus, life is easier when your dog is responsive to you and able to follow commands. Training is a lot of work, but once you understand the science behind successful dog training, it will be easier for you to understand how your dog's mind works.

Clear Expectations

One issue that dog owners face when training is setting clear expectations. If you're trying to teach your dog that begging at the kitchen table is bad, and another family member is slipping food scraps under the table, that person is undermining your attempts to teach your dog a house rule. When teaching your dog how to behave, every member of the household needs to abide by the same rules. Otherwise, your dog will receive mixed messages and become confused.

Even if you're the only human in your home, it's important to stick to the rules you made when you brought your puppy home. If your pup isn't allowed to jump on your couch, correct your dog each time he tries. Also make sure you don't invite your dog up for a special occasion; otherwise, you'll unravel all of the work you did to keep your dog off your furniture.

Clear expectations also apply to basic obedience training. If you're teaching your dog how to sit, standard practice says that the dog should receive the reward once the action is complete. This means that you should not praise your dog or give a treat until his bottom is on the floor and he holds that position. If you get hasty with your rewards and give your dog a treat when he's already off the ground, you're not reinforcing the behavior you ultimately want. The same applies for using consistent commands; if you use different words for the same action, your dog will become confused. For example, if you use both "down" and "off" for when you want your dog to get off someone or jump down from the furniture, he will have a hard time distinguishing between the two commands.

Dogs aren't great at reasoning and don't understand conditions like humans do. If you tell a child not to sit on your expensive couch because she's covered in mud, you can explain your reasoning. That way, the child knows that she's allowed to sit on the couch when she's clean, because you

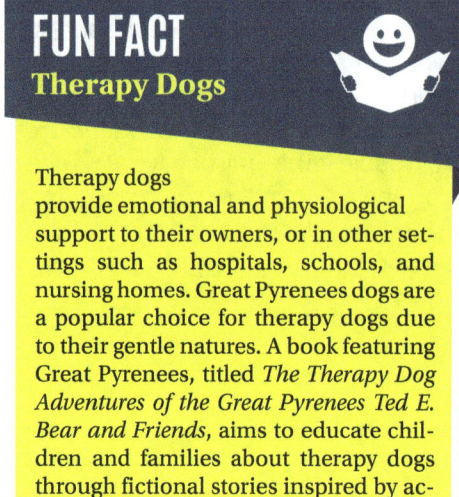

FUN FACT
Therapy Dogs

Therapy dogs provide emotional and physiological support to their owners, or in other settings such as hospitals, schools, and nursing homes. Great Pyrenees dogs are a popular choice for therapy dogs due to their gentle natures. A book featuring Great Pyrenees, titled *The Therapy Dog Adventures of the Great Pyrenees Ted E. Bear and Friends*, aims to educate children and families about therapy dogs through fictional stories inspired by actual therapy dog experiences.

don't want your couch to get dirty. Dogs can learn either that the couch is okay, or that it's forbidden. They don't understand in-between scenarios. Your Great Pyrenees will never understand that you like his company on the couch when he's clean, but you don't like when he makes a mess on your furniture. So, when you make rules, keep them simple and stick to them. When you choose a word for a command, stick to it. Dogs will not understand that different words can mean the same thing.

Operant Conditioning Basics

Dogs learn commands through operant conditioning. This is a psychological concept that is used to shape behaviors in both humans and canines. When the subject performs a behavior, this behavior is met with an outcome. A good outcome tells the subject to continue that behavior. A negative outcome tells the subject to avoid the behavior.

In one famous study of operant conditioning, rats were presented with a lever. When the rat pushed the lever, food was dispensed. As a result, the rats kept pushing the lever to get food, even if the food wasn't dispensed every time. In another part of the study, rats were presented with a lever that gave them a mild shock when they pressed it. As a result, the rats were conditioned to avoid the lever so they could prevent the unpleasant shock. Even tiny animals can learn that their actions have consequences; the rats' behaviors were shaped by their pleasure or aversion to whatever happened after the lever was pressed.

Dogs learn commands in the same way. If a reward is presented after completing a desired action, the dog will develop mental connections between the command, the action, and the reward. However, it takes a lot of repetition to strengthen this connection. A dog doesn't necessarily understand that "sit" means "put my bottom on the ground and wait for a treat." It takes a lot of time for your dog to build the connection between a combination of sounds to the correct action, which ultimately leads to the reward. Your dog doesn't necessarily understand or think about the meaning of your words, but with lots of practice, he will do the action automatically because he has been conditioned to do so.

Primary Reinforcements

Rewards are an extremely important part of operant conditioning. Most dogs are eager to please their humans, so any time your dog knows that he's doing something right, he'll be thrilled. Rewards can be broken down into two categories: primary reinforcements and secondary reinforcements.

Primary reinforcement is a reward that is good in and of itself. Treats and toys are two powerful rewards. Not every dog goes wild for treats, and others aren't interested in toys. But most dogs find one of these two rewards to be very powerful. If you're lucky, your dog will love both!

When choosing a reward, pick something that is special and highly enticing. For example, if you know your dog goes crazy for a specific flavor of dog treat, keep plenty of those high-value treats on hand. Moist treats tend to work better than dry because the water content makes the treat more appetizing to dogs as it gives off a stronger smell. Some owners will use small pieces of hot dog for training because they give off a strong aroma. When your dog gets tired of one flavor of treat, switch things up and try another. You'll be amazed at how excited your dog gets.

When rewarding your dog, make sure you don't give your reward too early or too late. If you give your reward before your dog completes the command, you will not be conditioning your dog to do the desired action. Similarly, if you give your dog the reward too late and he has broken the command, he will not make the connection between the action and the reward. It can be hard to use primary reinforcements when first starting out because your dog hasn't grasped the command well enough.

As your dog starts to get the hang of a command, you can change the schedule of reinforcement. Instead of giving a treat every time your dog sits, give a treat every third time. The theory is that your dog will continue to do the command because he knows a reward will come eventually. Or, he knows that if he returns the toy when playing fetch, his owner will allow him to tug and play with it for a little bit. Eventually, your dog will get to the point where you shouldn't need treats to get him to successfully complete a command.

Photo Courtesy of Brittany Alexandria Lewis

Secondary Reinforcements

Secondary reinforcements are rewards that can be exchanged for something inherently good. In the human world, money is a secondary reinforcement because paper and coins hold little value unless it can be exchanged for something personally valuable. Because dogs have no use for human currency, we have to create other types of "currency" dogs can find value in. Clicker training and using voice prompts are types of secondary rewards that can condition your dog to follow your commands.

Clicker training is popular with dog trainers because it is precise and doesn't require a ton of treats during training time. The clicker is a small, handheld device that makes a clicking sound when the button is pressed. This sound is supposed to serve as a reward to your dog, letting him know that he did something good. To associate those positive feelings with a sound, the dog must first be conditioned to understanding that the sound is the reward. This is done by clicking and giving the dog treats and praise. Over time, he will associate the sound with primary rewards and positive feelings.

Once your dog accepts the clicker as a reward, it's time to train. When your dog hits his mark, give a click. The clicker is instantaneous and lets your dog know that he's doing exactly what you want him to do in the moment. You can use the clicker along with treats to strengthen your dog's connection between primary and secondary reinforcements, but the clicker also allows you to quickly reward your dog without giving him too many treats in a short period of time.

If you don't have a clicker, your voice can have a similar effect. When your dog does something good, say, "yes" or "good" to reward your dog. Combine your chosen command with treats, just like you would if you were using a clicker, and you'll be able to reward your dog without treats or clicker devices. Make sure that you use a marker word that you don't use in another context with your pup so you don't cause confusion. This is a great tool to have when you find yourself in a teachable moment and don't have treats or a clicker on hand. For example, if your dog associates the word "yes" with a primary reinforcement, you can reward your dog with that word when taking your dog to the bathroom in the middle of the night.

Dangers of Punishment

"Great Pyrenees are a very sensitive breed. You can be too tough with a Pyrenees and they will just cower and break your heart. During training, I feel that it is best to have a firm voice but be repetitive in your commands. In my experience, training with treats for positive reinforcement works much better than negative reinforcement."

Lindsey Morrison
Golden Pond Farms

Punishment is a type of reinforcement that should not be used in training because it can deliver unpredictable results, and dogs generally don't respond well to punishment. Great Pyrenees are fairly sensitive dogs, so they are not likely to respond well to punishments of any sort. Not only is punishment less effective than positive reinforcement, but it is often carried out using cruel methods. A dog owner should shape positive behaviors, not punish dogs for acting like dogs.

Punishment is different from correction because it uses more extreme methods to get a point across. For example, when correcting a dog, you make a noise to get his attention so you can guide his in the right direction. Punishment is making a noise intended to scare or intimidate an animal. There is a difference between a firm "no" and screaming at your dog. Berating your dog when he makes mistakes will not teach him to act better. In fact, you're likely to make your dog fear you. Dogs learn best when they're eager to please, not terrified of upsetting you.

Pain is another form of punishment that should be avoided at all costs. Even if you think swatting at your dog doesn't cause a lot of harm, the psychological effects are long-lasting. In the past, dog owners might have swatted a dog on the bottom or nose for misbehaving, but this can cause your dog to be afraid of you. If the fear is serious enough, the dog may lash out and injure someone. When someone hurts or scares a dog into behaving, that person creates all sorts of aversions in that dog. Sometimes, you'll see adopted dogs with strange fears because the dog had bad experiences with a type of person or object, and the dog carries that fear for the rest of his life.

In some cases, punishment creates worse behaviors. It's not uncommon for inexperienced puppy owners to push a dog's face in his poop while scolding him because people believe that it will teach him not to have accidents. Little do they know, a dog can't connect the past experience of having an accident with the present experience of being yelled at and pushed around. However, the dog may think that there's a connection between going potty and punishment, so he might then find more private places to use the bathroom in the house.

Avoid punishing your dog at all costs. A dog's brain is not complex enough to fully understand why someone is intimidating, scaring, or hurting him. While punishment is a part of operant conditioning, and has its place when it comes to shaping human behaviors, it's not very effective on dogs and can ultimately lead to more unwanted behaviors. Use positive reinforcement as much as possible and your dog will want to please you. Great Pyrenees can be stubborn at times, but this breed loves to make its owners happy.

Photo Courtesy of Amy M Gates - Stroud

Photo Courtesy of Shelly Bergeson

CHAPTER 10 Training Your Great Pyrenees

Hiring a Trainer and Attending Classes

"I recommend putting them in puppy class, and then continuing with dog training classes after that as well. They should know the basic commands which are sit, stay, heel, down, stay, wait and leave it, Leave it is very important because if they pick up something (like a chicken bone) which is dangerous, they will drop it for you."

Susie Wong
Darlington Great Pyrenees

There are multiple benefits to working with a professional, experienced dog trainer. When you take a class, the trainer is teaching you how to work with your dog as much as the trainer is teaching the dog. The trainer will learn about your individual needs and help you find ways to get through to your unique dog.

When you take a group class, your dog has the opportunity to practice while interacting with different people and animals. When dogs only practice commands in a familiar place, with familiar people, they miss out on all of the distractions needed to really challenge them. If you want your dog to be able to complete commands in real-world settings, you need to practice in real-world settings. Your dog will have the opportunity to socialize and practice in a challenging setting in a class, as opposed to only practicing in your kitchen.

A trainer is also a good all-around resource to have in your life when it comes to raising a dog. An experienced trainer has worked with a lot of dogs and knows about different behavioral traits. If you're at a loss for why your dog acts the way he does, a trainer can listen to your issues and help you work out a solution. Trainers are also well-connected in the dog world, so if your trainer can't answer a question or provide a specific type of training, she'll know someone else who does.

When looking for a trainer, choose someone with experience. Experience with Great Pyrenees is a plus. Pick a trainer who uses positive reinforcement. If your trainer uses punishment or intimidation tactics with their dogs, avoid them. Choose someone who is friendly and loves dogs. You want to build a working relationship with this person so you can go to them with any questions you may have. A trainer who is happy to give out their phone number or email address and will answer questions without charging you extra is a safe bet. You want a trainer who you feel comfortable with because you're trusting them to give you the right advice for training your dog.

Photo Courtesy of Brittany Alexandria Lewis

CHAPTER 10   Training Your Great Pyrenees

Owner Behavior

While a dog's behavior is the main focus when it comes to training, an owner's behavior is also important. Dogs feed off human emotions, especially sensitive dogs. If a human is calm and positive, the dog will look to them to know how to feel, and will realize that everything is okay. If the owner is anxious, frustrated, or angry, the dog will sense that something is wrong, and will also be on high alert. A calm voice tells your dog that you're calm. A high-pitched voice or an angry voice will make your dog excited or upset. Training happens best when everyone is calm and ready to work.

Training a dog is no easy task. It's natural to get frustrated when your dog isn't picking up on a command. It's also frustrating when you're doing what the trainer tells you and your dog is still uninterested in obeying. If you ever find yourself getting frustrated during training time, stop and return to it once you've calmed down. There's no point in making the practice unpleasant for either you or your dog. Make training sessions short so neither of you get fatigued, and make sure you play with your dog after training time is over. Training should be a fun, positive, experience and not a chore. If you dread having to work with your dog, find a fun class to take with your pup or talk to your trainer about making training more enjoyable.

Once you understand the science behind dog training, you can apply it to any activity. Conditioning requires repetition; even if you think you've mastered a command on the first day, you'll need to practice it for at least a few weeks in different settings until your dog can perform the command reliably. Make sure you have plenty of rewards and avoid punishment at all costs. Training is a lot of work, but once your dog has mastered a few basic commands, you'll be glad you spent the time.

CHAPTER 11
Basic Commands

While there are tons of tricks to teach your dog, some are more important than others. It's fun to have a dog that rolls over on command, but it's not practical for everyday situations. Basic commands help a dog owner keep their pup under control. Dogs have a lot of natural instincts, but these don't always apply to the human world that they can't quite understand. Therefore, it is the responsibility of the owner to keep dogs safe. One great way to do that is to equip your dog with a basic set of commands so you can prevent naughty or dangerous behavior. This chapter will explain why these commands are so important, and give you step by step directions for teaching your dog.

Benefits of Proper Training

Safety is perhaps the biggest reason obedience training is necessary. It can be hard to predict how a dog will act in different scenarios, so it's important to have some control. Great Pyrenees are known for their sense of adventure, so it's not unlikely that yours will try to test his boundaries. If your dog is running down the street, you need to be able to get him to return to you and to stay still long enough to clip on a leash. Otherwise, you risk losing your dog or having him injured in an accident.

The Great Pyrenees is a large breed that can do a lot of damage. Your dog may jump up on someone out of affection and excitement, but if he jumps on someone smaller or weaker, your dog could hurt someone. It's useful to know commands that can call your dog off someone if he's already jumped up, or to keep him calm and still when you know he's going to be excited.

If left unchecked, the Great Pyrenees is likely to make his own rules around the house. As stated in an earlier chapter, the owner should be the pack leader, not the dog. If you have no means of controlling your dog, you will soon grow frustrated by his behavior.

For example, this breed is known for being protective. When someone rings your doorbell, or simply walks past your house, your dog will want to warn you. As thoughtful as this is, most of these warnings are completely unnecessary. Over time, this barking and general excitement may drive you crazy. So, if you don't practice staying calm with your dog, or you don't have tools available to keep your dog quiet when necessary, you may soon grow frustrated by his need to alert you to every insignificant sound or movement outside your door.

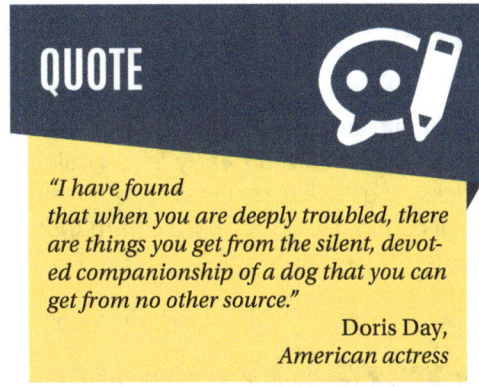

"I have found that when you are deeply troubled, there are things you get from the silent, devoted companionship of a dog that you can get from no other source."

Doris Day, American actress

Learning a few basic commands won't automatically turn your dog into a model canine citizen, but it should help with some unwanted behaviors. These commands will also help you take your dog out into the world and interact with others. Training is also a great mental exercise for a motivated dog, and will keep your pup entertained as you work on commands. There are so many benefits to teaching your dog basic commands. The repetition of training may feel monotonous at times, but all of the time and effort you put into training will be worth it in the end.

Places to Practice

When training your dog, your surroundings matter. Your dog may be able to sit and stay in the quiet of your own home, but try it for the first time in a busy dog park, and you'll see that all of your practice has gone out the window. It's natural for a dog to become very distracted by his surroundings, making it very difficult to listen to your commands. That's why it's good to practice in a variety of settings so your dog will reliably respond to your commands.

When first starting out, you'll probably want to practice in a familiar place with few distractions. Your home is a great place to start. Once you've mastered a command inside, move to your backyard. This space will be familiar enough to set your dog up for success, but just distracting enough to provide an added challenge. From there, find different places around town to practice the same commands. A natural progression may involve a quiet park, a friend's house, and a busy, but familiar dog park. When your dog has gotten good at a few particular commands, find a very distracting place to practice. A busy outdoor market or mall may be a good place to test leash skills or a sit and stay.

Have realistic expectations for your dog and set him up for success. If you master a skill in the backyard, you can't always expect your dog to perform at a busy dog park. If your dog has a tough time following directions in one location, don't give up! Your dog may just need more time to practice the skill, more time to get used to the location, or more time to mature. Set goals and keep working toward them at a reasonable pace.

Basic Commands

There's a reason basic dog training classes focus on sit and down and not shake and play dead—there are some skills that can be extremely useful to learn from an early age. While there is always time to practice fun tricks, you'll want to save those for after you've built a foundation of practical commands. These are commands that will help you keep your big dog under control and safe.

Sit

Photo Courtesy of Jessica Rittenhouse

This is perhaps the first command you will ever teach your dog. "Sit" is useful for controlling your Great Pyrenees and keeping him still. You can practice this command while waiting to cross the street, when someone comes to the door, or while talking to people at the park.

To teach this command, start with your dog standing in front of you, facing you. Hold a treat in front of his nose, then slowly move it up and back. He will naturally sit in order to reach the treat. The second his bottom touches the floor, say, "Yes! Good sit!" and give him the treat. Eventually, your dog will understand that the "sit" command means he is supposed to sit until given further instruction. When you're ready for your dog to get up, say "okay" and have him stand and come toward you. Repeat this motion and connect the verbal command to the action until he can hear the "sit" command and do what you want.

If you're having difficulties getting your dog into this position, you might want to apply light pressure above the base of his tail to gently move him into the sit position. You're not forcing your Great Pyrenees down, but gently reminding him what you mean by "sit." Also, if your dog is not responding, don't repeat the command until he listens. Say "sit" once, then if he doesn't respond, either move the treat in front of his face, or apply light pressure on his bottom until he catches on.

CHAPTER 11   Basic Commands

Stay

This command is necessary if you have a Great Pyrenees who wants to explore everything. Because this breed is known for wandering, training for this command will give you some peace of mind to know that your dog isn't going to bolt the second you turn your back. If your dog can sit and stay, you won't have to worry about him running off if you have to drop the leash for a moment. It's also good to know if you want to play hide and seek with your dog. Begin by teaching this command in the sit position, then move to the down position.

Start with your dog sitting beside you, facing the same direction. Say "stay" and hold your hand in front of his face.

Photo Courtesy of Angel Scott

If he doesn't move after a brief moment, reward him. Once he has mastered that, try walking in a circle around your dog. The second he moves, put him back into the sit position and try again. Don't reward your dog if he does so much as flinch, but give lots of praise and rewards if he manages to stay still.

Once your dog has the basic idea, create more distance between you and him. Have him stay, then back away, then return. Or, have him stay, then call him to you. Add more distance and distractions to test your dog's ability to listen and trust you. At the beginning, set your dog up for success by keeping the wait time and the distance between you short. As your dog's skills develop, add more space, time, and distractions.

Down

This command puts your dog in a prone position. This might be a bit harder to teach a Great Pyrenees than sit, because your stubborn dog may see this as a submissive position. But it's a good one to teach, because it tells your dog that you need him to relax for a little while. For instance, you might have your dog sit when you need him to be still for just a moment,

Photo Courtesy of Melanie Hollingworth

like if you need to clip a leash on him. In contrast, you might put your dog in a down position when you need him out of the way for a longer period of time, like if someone is at the door and he's very anxious about visitors.

To teach this, start with your dog in the seated position. Then take your treat and hold it in front of the dog's nose. Lower the treat to the ground, and with any luck, your dog's head should follow it until his chin is near the ground. You can also tuck your fingers into your dog's collar or gently apply tension to his leash so his head lowers to the floor. When his elbows touch the ground, say, "Yes! Good down!" and give him the treat. Never use excessive force to position your dog on the ground.

Come

The recall command can be very useful when a sudden danger appears, or you just want your dog to come inside at the end of the day. This command is particularly useful for Great Pyrenees owners because this dog can be an escape artist. If you catch your dog in the process of running off, a strong recall can keep him from straying too far. The end goal is to have your dog stop on a dime and return to you, no matter how focused he is on his adventure. For example, if your dog starts to chase a stray cat into the street, a dog with good recall skills will immediately turn and race back to you when he hears "come."

CHAPTER 11 Basic Commands

Take a very yummy treat and excitedly say your dog's name. If he comes running to you to investigate, say "Yes! Good come!" and reward him. Or, if your dog naturally comes to you, reward him in the same way as if you purposefully called him. Increase the distance and continue calling your dog and rewarding with tasty treats. Over time, you'll want to get to the point where you can touch your dog's collar without him jumping back and running away. Some dogs can't resist being chased, so you'll want to make sure your dog will come to you without trying to get you to give chase. Adding the sit command will help you hold onto him in case of emergency. Once your dog begins to understand "come," try adding a sit and stay to keep him from dashing off again to play.

Sometimes owners call their dog because an animal has been naughty. When this happens, the owner's voice is usually harsh and angry. This teaches the dog that if he responds to "come," he will be punished. Only use the come command in positive situations, or your dog may not obey when it really counts. You want your dog to think that coming to you is the best thing in the world, and that he'll be met with lot of love and affection.

Photo Courtesy of Jenni Fellman

Drop It

Photo Courtesy of Jessica Rittenhouse

This skill may not be on the top of the list of basic skills owners teach their new dogs, but it can save a dog's life in an emergency. Dogs are naturally curious, so they're inclined to put their mouths on things they find enticing or interesting. Many times, the things they find can make them sick, like a rotting animal or a forbidden food. Sometimes it's also worth it to teach this command just so you can successfully play fetch and not spend half of your time chasing your dog to get the ball back.

If you play catch or fetch with your Great Pyrenees, this is a perfect way to teach the command. Toss and ball and let him catch it in his mouth. If he drops the ball on his own, praise this behavior—"Good drop!" If your dog is not so willing to relinquish his toy, hold a treat in front of his face. He will likely drop the ball so there is room for a treat in his mouth. Praise this behavior in the same way you would if he dropped it without prompting. For play-driven dogs, your pup may just want an opportunity to tug at the toy before dropping it. As long as your dog eventually drops it, a quick tug can be a good reward for bringing an object to you. Eventually, you'll be able to tell your dog to pick up and object and put it back down without rewards. If you ever catch your dog with something gross in his mouth, you'll be glad he learned this command.

Walk

Because Great Pyrenees require exercise, going on walks is a necessary part of life. This is a strong dog that can pull you around and make walks very unpleasant if your dog doesn't willingly walk by your side. Walking nicely on the leash is not intuitive to most dogs. They would much rather run ahead or lag behind as they sniff and explore every new smell. What you're aiming for is what is often referred to as a "heel." This means that your dog walks close to you with a loose leash.

Always walk with your dog on your left side. This routine teaches your dog that he belongs in a specific place and should not be wandering. Hold the end of the leash in your right hand and slide your left hand halfway down

CHAPTER 11   Basic Commands

the leash to keep your dog close. That way, if your dog gets out of position, the tension on the leash will correct him. To teach your dog to stay close on your left hip, hold a treat in your right hand, guiding him forward with the treat. If he walks with you, give him tons of praise and treats. If your dog looks at you for direction at any point, make a big deal about how great of a job he is doing. You want your dog to walk with you, rather than attempting to lead. This is especially important when your dog could easily pull you around. If your full-sized dog pulls hard enough, you may be injured.

Great Pyrenees are strong dogs with thick, fluffy necks and may not care if there is tension on the leash. Instead, they will surge ahead, even to the point where it hurts their throat. One way to alert your dog that this behavior is not acceptable is to stop in your tracks the moment he starts to pull. Over time, he will figure out that he can only receive his reward if he walks with a loose leash. If that's not enough, do an abrupt about-turn every time he pulls. It may be a while before you actually go anywhere, but it will teach your Great Pyrenees that you're in charge of the walk. Some owners will switch to a harness in fear that a dog will hurt himself, but this will sometimes just allow a dog to pull harder, because a harness doesn't hurt. Ideally, you should be able to walk your Great Pyrenees with a buckle collar. If walking on a leash is a problem for your dog, talk to a trainer about how you can rectify the situation. Because this dog is so big and strong, you'll want someone with experience to help you remedy the problem.

Because it's easy for bad walking habits to manifest in your Great Pyrenees, it's important to be strict when it comes to leash training. Don't allow your dog to pull, just for the sake of exercise. You may find yourself spinning in circles for a few walks, but it's better than allowing your dog to drag you for every walk in the future. Never go on a walk without plenty of treats, because every walk is full of training opportunities. Don't give up on going on walks because your Great Pyrenees has a mind of his own. Keep working at it until your dog obediently walks with a loose leash.

Photo Courtesy of Emily Sharon Thompson

Watch Me

Teaching your dog to look you in the eye is a very subtle command that instills good habits in your Great Pyrenees. This dog has a mind of its own, so he needs frequent reminders that you're in charge, and that he needs to look to you for direction. This skill is very beneficial when it comes to going on walks or avoiding distractions. It's also useful when you want to take the perfect picture of your Great Pyrenees!

Photo Courtesy of Shelby Brewer

CHAPTER 11   Basic Commands

Start by having your dog sit in front of you. Say, "Watch me" and hold a treat in each hand, with your hands by your eyes. When your dog's gaze meets the treats (or your eyes) say, "Yes!" and give them a treat. Repeat this until your dog looks at you when he hears the command even when there's not a treat in front of your face. Once you've mastered this, practice it when your dog is in a sit and stay with lots of distractions. Wait for your pup to track a squirrel with his eyes and then say the command. If he looks to you, then you know he's mastered it! One challenge of dog training is grabbing your dog's attention, so if you make a practice of teaching your dog to consistently pay attention to you, training will be much easier.

These seven commands are just the start of your dog training adventure. Once you master these commands, build off these skills and teach more challenging ones. If your dog can do these seven commands, you'll feel comfortable taking your dog into new situations and letting him out of your sight for short periods of time. Also, you'll find that your dog is easier to manage and your household will be less hectic than it was when your crazy dog was running wild. Remember to use positive reinforcement and repetition when you teach each of these skills. When your dog starts to get the hang of a command, take him to a new location with new distractions and continue your practice. With regular practice, your dog will be a breeze to take care of.

CHAPTER 12
Advanced Commands

"Mine have always been easy to train with treats, but many have their quirks. My male hates to be on his back. He learned to sit and lay down, but he does it at his own speed, since males can be slower the older they get. However, he hates to be on his back and will not for any reason roll over, even though my female will fly on her back at the chance of a treat. With repetition and a reward system, they usually are quick to learn. I knew someone once that trained their farm Pyrs that they would not get pet until they sat. These two giants would come racing down the pasture and sit on a dime at the feet of their owner so they would get pet."

Lindsey Morrison
Golden Pond Farms

FUN FACT
Best in Show

As of 2019, a Great Pyrenees has never been awarded the Best in Show title at the Westminster Kennel Club Dog Show. In 2005, the Great Pyrenees, Ch. Dieudonne Impyrial Acclaim, took home the trophy for the Working Group at the Westminster Dog Show.

Once you've mastered the basic commands, it's time to begin a new challenge. Dog tricks are only limited by your imagination and your dog's willingness to learn. It's a lot of fun to show your friends and family all of the cool tricks your dog can perform. Obedience training is a good way to exercise your dog's body and mind, so even if you feel as though you've taught your dog all of the necessary commands, it's good to keep practicing the old tricks and continuing to add new tricks to your dog's repertoire. Here are a few commands that are popular with dog owners.

CHAPTER 12   Advanced Commands

Play Dead

Photo Courtesy of Michele Morgan

If your dog knows "down" then you are on your way to teaching play dead. When your dog is in the down position, hold a treat in front of his nose, and slowly turn your hand in a circle, going over his head. His head should follow your hand to the point where he ends up on his side. When he gets into the "dead" position, mark his good behavior and use your command name. You can choose a silly command name like "dead dog!" or "bang!" How lifeless or ridiculous your dog looks depends upon how you move your hand to manipulate his body. With some trial and error, you'll be able to position your dog however you want.

Roll Over

Photo Courtesy of Alicia Klocek

Roll over is very similar to play dead. For roll over, your dog just needs to be able to complete the roll he started with play dead. However, some dogs are resistant to rolling over and will need lots of practice. Rolling over can be a sign of submission in dogs, so no matter how many times you practice, some dogs will really resist rolling all the way over. If you get the motion down for each of these variations from the down position, try to start from a seated position for a greater challenge, or get him to pop back up to a sit after rolling over.

Crawl

Photo Courtesy of Brittany McDowell & Steven Vail

This trick is adorable because your dog will scoot along the ground on his belly, wiggling his fluffy bottom. Start your dog in a down position and hold a treat on the ground, just out of reach. Your dog will start to move forward to get the treat. If he stands up, don't give him the reward. Try again until your dog crawls forward a few steps before rewarding him. Once he gets the hang of it, increase the distance. For added difficulty, have your dog crawl under an object or between your legs.

Spin

Photo Courtesy of Nancy Bierley

Getting your dog to twirl around for a treat makes him look like he's dancing. Your Great Pyrenees will be too big to dance with you on hind legs, so this is a good way to get him to dance without having him balance his heavy body on your shoulders. Have your dog face you in a standing position. Hold a treat in your hand and call your dog over. When your dog is about to take the treat, bring the treat in toward your body, then out and around in a circle. Your dog will follow your hand and spin as you make a circle with your arm. It's best to get a little momentum going into the spin, so try to call your dog to you, so he has built up enough speed to complete the turn. When you've mastered right turns, try left turns. You can also alternate directions or add other movements into your dance.

CHAPTER 12   Advanced Commands

Shake

Photo Courtesy of Marisa Alford

This is a classic dog trick, but be advised when you teach this trick to your dog as a little puppy. Your little pup has a small paw, so you won't get hurt if he paws at you. However, your puppy will grow up to be a very large dog, and a big paw can cause some damage. So if you teach your Great Pyrenees this trick, make sure he only performs the trick when prompted. Some dogs learn that shaking equals a treat, so they'll put a paw up when they want a snack. If you're worried about your adult dog whacking people with his massive paws, skip this trick and try another.

To teach this trick, have your dog sit facing you. Hold a treat in your hand, near the paw you want him to lift. He will likely sniff and push your hand with his nose out of curiosity, but don't give him the treat just yet. When he can't force it out of your hand, he will use this paw to try and open your hand. If he tries to use his paw in any way, say the command and give him the treat. Continue this until your dog responds to the command by lifting his paw for you to grab. If he doesn't respond to the treat in your hand, you may try poking at the foot or leg until he lifts it. Praise and reward this behavior when it happens.

These are just a few suggestions of fun tricks to try. If you need more inspiration, talk to other dog owners or dog trainers about fun tricks they like to teach their dogs. If you're feeling creative, you can even come up with your own tricks that mesh well with your dog's personality and abilities. If you know how to effectively train a dog and how to manipulate behaviors with treats, there's no limit to what your dog can do!

CHAPTER 13
Dealing with Unwanted Behaviors

"The two behaviors I warn new owners about are: 1) putting their big paw up on you as though they're trying to shake your hand, or 2) jumping up on you. Those are very unwanted behaviors and should never be allowed no matter how cute the puppy looks doing them."

Susan Grimm
Grimm Acres, Diversified

Dogs are a lot of fun—until they start acting up! Dogs like to make up their own rules and at one point or another, your Great Pyrenees will do something you don't like. Because dogs are trainable, you may be able to correct these bad behaviors and turn them into something more productive. However, it can be challenging when your dog has a natural tendency to be naughty. This chapter will cover some common bad behaviors in dogs and give you ideas for solutions.

CHAPTER 13   Dealing with Unwanted Behaviors

What Is Bad Behavior in Dogs?

Bad behavior can be hard to define. After all, it isn't as though your dog is being malicious when he jumps up to say hello—he just doesn't know that he's too big to jump on people. Or, your dog may have the best intentions of keeping you safe when he barks at everything that moves, and he has no idea he's annoying your neighbors and you wish he would be quieter. If you could talk to your dog, he'd probably say that it's unfair that you get upset with him for just being a dog, and he might remind you that his ancestors never had to use the bathroom in one particular place. Your dog needs to learn how to follow your rules, but it will take time, patience, and lots of practice.

Unwanted behaviors can be grouped into three categories: annoying, destructive, and dangerous. Chances are, anything your dog does that you don't like will fit into one of those categories. There is a difference in severity among the three. Annoying behaviors, like barking, aren't typically harmful and are often ignored. However, your relationship with your dog can certainly take a negative turn if you must constantly listen to loud barking. If you stop such behavior before it becomes a bad habit, your relationship with your Great Pyrenees will be much better.

Destructive behaviors are ones that damage your belongings and property. These are harder to ignore because your dog can cause a lot of harm to your home, yard, or personal belongings. Chewing and digging are examples of activities that dogs love, but owners hate. If you can catch your dog in the act, you can redirect his behavior and help him find something else that is more rewarding than chewing your shoes. You can't supervise your dog 100 percent of the time but you can teach him how to behave when you're not around.

Finally, there are some unwanted behaviors that can be outright dangerous. Chasing other animals and aggression toward people are behaviors you want to correct immediately so no one gets hurt. Some dogs have high prey drives and want to hunt any furry creature that gives chase. This isn't a big deal when your furry friend is chasing rabbits out of your garden, but it's not safe if you have a cat that your dog loves to torment. Or, your Great Pyrenees may be fearful of certain types of people, to the point where he feels like he needs to defend himself or others by growling or nipping. Annoying behaviors can be ignored and destroyed objects can be replaced, but an injury to a person or animal at the hands of your pet can create lasting damage for everyone involved. These are issues that must be dealt with immediately.

Any behavior that is not compatible with your daily life can be considered "bad" behavior. Once you decide which behaviors you will allow and which behaviors cannot be tolerated, it's time to train your dog how to live in your home. Consider focusing on the most disruptive behaviors first, then moving on to the more harmless, but slightly irritating behaviors as your dog learns his place in the world.

Finding the Root of the Problem

> "You can take my heart, but I can't let you take my dog."
> — Karin Slaughter, American writer

Successful dog trainers have the ability to think like a dog. Once you observe your dog for a while, you'll start to understand his motivations for some of what he does, even if certain behavior remains baffling.

You may not understand why your dog insists on jumping on you, even when you scold him. But, when you stop and think about what reward your dog may get from the action, you'll understand. When your dog gets excited and wants you to notice him, he jumps up on people because it's a proven method of getting a human's attention. Even when you scold your dog and make him jump down, he's still rewarded by the attention you give him. So, if you want to teach your dog not to jump, you have to figure out why he jumps and take away the reward. Instead of grabbing his paws and setting them on the ground, you may anticipate his movements and turn your back when he jumps, ignoring him. Over time, he'll learn that there is no longer a reward for jumping on people, so he should find another method to get pets, like sitting and waiting patiently.

Or, you may be at a loss as to why your dog randomly digs holes in your yard. When you observe his behavior for a while, you might notice that he only digs holes under bushes in the summer. Therefore, you can safely assume that your hot Great Pyrenees is trying to create a den so he can cool off. In order to prevent this behavior in the future, you might try to correct him when you catch him in the act, set up barriers in his favorite digging spots, or leave him inside with air conditioning on hot days.

Many problem behaviors are a result of a dog's natural instincts. Before immediately dismissing your dog as "naughty," try to get down to his level and figure out the motivation behind his actions. That way, you'll be more likely to find an effective way to redirect or correct his unwanted behaviors.

CHAPTER 13   Dealing with Unwanted Behaviors

Bad Behavior Prevention

The best time to correct your dog's unwanted behaviors is as soon as you notice them. This is easier said than done, but it will save you time and energy if you correct your dog from an early age, rather than requiring him to unlearn bad habits later. For instance, there's a very good reason dog owners potty train puppies from the minute they come home. If you allow your dog to use your house as a bathroom until he's a year old, he'll believe that he's allowed to go wherever he pleases. Once that behavior settles in your dog's brain, it will be much harder to convince him to wait to potty outside than relieve himself whenever he feels the urge. So, to prevent messes, it's important to practice good housetraining skills early on.

Some bad behaviors can be avoided altogether if your dog never learns them in the first place. Begging is a very annoying behavior that can be hard to break because your dog believes he will get tasty treats if he climbs up on your table and whines. But if you never offer your dog food from the table, or offer him people food at all, he will be less likely to think that he's missing out on something because he's never received a reward for begging.

Photo Courtesy of Jessica Tyre

115

Photo Courtesy of Leigha Nichter

CHAPTER 13   Dealing with Unwanted Behaviors

Regular obedience training can also help to keep your pooch in check. If your dog can sit, lie down, stay, and come on command, then you'll have some control. This can come in handy when you know your dog is about to act up. For instance, if your dog has a bad habit of storming the door when visitors arrive, you can tell him to lie down on his bed when you hear the doorbell. That way, he doesn't have the chance to be rewarded with attention when someone opens the door.

Another way to prevent bad behavior is to tend to your dog's needs. For instance, if your puppy chews on all of your belongings, it's probably because he's bored or teething, and needs something to gnaw on. Leaving a puppy home alone without a chew toy is a recipe for disaster.

The frequency with which you take your dog outside can also prevent accidents, another common bad behavior. If you take your puppy outside at least once an hour, he'll have more chances to go to the bathroom in the correct spot.

If your dog just has too much energy to behave, take him outside to play. By the time you're done, your dog will be too tired to be naughty.

Bad habits can be hard to break, especially with a stubborn dog like a Great Pyrenees. The more time you spend training your dog, the better off he'll be, especially if you start early.

How to Properly Correct Your Dog

When you catch your dog doing something naughty, you must teach him that the behavior isn't acceptable. To do this, you need to witness the behavior so you can get the dog's attention and redirect him on the spot. If you come home, notice a mess, and scold your dog, he won't remember or understand he did something that you don't like.

When people correct their dog's bad behavior, some make the mistake of using punishment, either in the form of pain or fear. This may change your dog's behavior, but it can also make him react poorly. When dogs get scared or agitated, they are liable to nip, growl, or bite. Even if they don't reach that point of distress, they may still cower and hide from you when you want to train them. In some cases, dogs continue with the bad behavior, but make sure to do it when you're away.

Correction is not the same as punishment, and it can still be a positive form of training. First, get your dog's attention. A clap or firm "hey!" should be enough to refocus his attention off his naughty activity and onto you.

Once you've got his attention, say "no!" and find a more productive use of his energy or attention. For example, if your dog is chewing on your shoe, get his attention, tell him no, take your shoe away, and direct him to a dog bone. When he takes the bone, praise him. If your dog is barking at the open window, get his attention and tell him "no!" Then distract him from the thing he finds rewarding by closing the blinds or calling him to you. When he takes a brief break from barking, praise him for being calm and quiet.

It's important to also "catch" your dog doing something good and give him tons of praise. For example, if your dog is a barker and you catch him in a quiet moment, say, "Good no bark!" and give him lots of love. If you catch your dog picking up a chew toy instead of the remote, praise him. Dogs react the best when given positive reinforcement, so even breaking bad habits should incorporate rewards.

Photo Courtesy of Alicia Klocek

CHAPTER 13   Dealing with Unwanted Behaviors

When to Call a Professional

Sometimes there's only so much an owner can do alone. Especially if you don't have a lot of experience working with dogs, there may be times where it is necessary to defer training to a pro. If you feel like you've tried every trick in the book and your dog is still exhibiting problem behavior, there is no shame in calling in backup. For example, if you've spent months trying to train your dog to walk nicely on a leash, but have made no progress and are on the verge of giving up, talk to a professional dog trainer about it. They may be able to come up with a solution that will make going on walks exponentially more pleasant.

If your dog is behaving in a way that is downright dangerous, like being aggressive toward others, it's crucial that you immediately talk to a vet, trainer, or other animal behavior specialist. It can be hard to pinpoint why a dog is being aggressive. A veterinarian visit can ensure that the problem isn't medical. Once the dog's health is cleared, talk to a trainer that has experience with working with aggressive dogs. The trainer should be able to diagnose the problem and give you tips for helping your dog feel more comfortable so he doesn't react poorly around people or other animals.

Even if the bad behaviors aren't serious, it never hurts to work with a professional trainer. Correcting unwanted behaviors can take some trial and error, especially for a novice owner, so a trainer can give you lots of tips for turning your dog into the perfect canine citizen.

It's not reasonable to expect your puppy to be perfect all the time. Great Pyrenees have a mind of their own, which won't always line up with your expectations. When you notice a bad behavior, try to deal with it as soon as you can, in a positive manner. Never punish your dog for bad behavior—instead, show him how you want him to behave and reward him for the good behavior. Dogs make great companions, but they don't automatically know how to live alongside a human. Therefore, it's the owner's responsibility to show the dog how he is expected to behave. Once those expectations are practiced, it doesn't take long for the dog to fit into the family.

CHAPTER 14
Traveling with Great Pyrenees

"My Pyrenees love to go for rides and will load themselves into the vehicle with a simple command. This is very helpful for vet visits as well as companionship on a road trip. Their sheer size makes other forms of travel complicated. Many people are uncomfortable with large dogs around. But, on the other hand, when I travel alone I love to take along one of my Pyrenees because they will provide a good early warning system for anyone approaching the vehicle and discourages any one from coming close to me without an invitation."

Susan Grimm
Grimm Acres, Diversified

CHAPTER 14   Traveling with Great Pyrenees

Once you've become attached to your pup, you won't want to go anywhere without him. A Great Pyrenees definitely can't be carried on an airplane or stowed in a handheld carrier in a hotel room. Because this dog is so massive, you'll need to make sure you're well prepared before going on any kind of trip with him. This chapter will give you some things to consider when planning a trip with your dog.

Crates and Car Restraints

Oftentimes, dog owners don't think to restrain their dog, even if they enforce seatbelt use in their vehicle. This is problematic for several reasons. First of all, a large dog can cause a lot of damage or can be badly injured in a crash. Secondly, dogs pose a major distraction while driving, if the dog is not restrained in the backseat. An unrestrained dog poses a safety danger to everyone in the car, not just the animal itself.

If your Great Pyrenees is crate trained, this is a perfect restraint that will keep your dog comfortable during your drive. If your car is large enough, you can place the crate somewhere the crate is secure and won't slide around. In the event of a crash, the crate will keep your dog from going flying, and it will protect him from getting hit with debris.

> **FUN FACT**
> **A Royal History**
>
> Great Pyrenees dogs originated as humble farm dogs in the Pyrenees mountains, but during the reign of Louis XIV were elevated in status and named the royal dog of France in 1675. Due to the fashionable nature of the breed, it was soon in demand with European nobility. During the 19th century, a Great Pyrenees named Gabbas was gifted to Queen Victoria of England. A portrait of Gabbas, commissioned by the queen, remains in the collection of Her Majesty the Queen.

If your dog isn't comfortable in a crate, or your car can't fit a crate, a safety harness is also a good choice. Pet stores sell seatbelts that look like short leashes. These allow you to clip your dog into your car's seatbelt and attach the other end to a collar or harness. A harness works well for large dogs like Great Pyrenees because it can distribute the force put on your dog's neck in the event of an accident. This type of restraint is adjustable, so you can make it comfortable for your dog without allowing him to jump into the front seat to say hello.

Preparing Your Dog for Car Rides

Some dogs love car rides and will immediately jump in the car whenever they have the chance. Others are hesitant to hop in the car and panic when the vehicle is in motion or get carsick. To build a positive connection between your dog and the car, it's good to take things slow and give positive reinforcement.

If you shove a nervous puppy into the car without warning, he may associate car rides with negative feelings. On the other hand, if you gently allow your dog to sniff out the car and explore for a little, then give treats and praise when he's calm, it will be easier for him to adjust to life on the road. When helping your dog get used to the car, give him time to check out the vehicle while it's parked. Once your dog can handle it, drive a short distance and give him lots of praise and treats. As your dog adjusts to being in a moving vehicle, lengthen your trips until your pup is as cool as a cucumber. Try not to make all your car trips to scary places, like the vet. That's a good way to make your dog fear car rides because he then associates the vehicle with something negative that is always going to happen.

Photo Courtesy of Shelby Brewer

If your dog is the type to get carsick, try to reduce his anxiety. Give him time to exercise before a trip so he's not overexcited. Put a familiar blanket or toy in the car to make him feel secure. If you think your dog's carsickness is unrelated to anxiety, talk to a vet about medication or supplements. While you figure out what is making your dog sick, waterproof seat protectors can keep your car interior from needing emergency detailing.

Flying and Hotel Stays

Depending on the length of your travels, air travel may be necessary. Because Great Pyrenees are so large, most airlines will not permit this breed to ride in the cabin. This means that your dog will need to travel in the plane's cargo hold with checked baggage. Not all dogs tolerate air travel, so you'll need to think about your dog's best interests before flying.

Your dog will need to be in a crate clearly labeled with your contact information. Familiar blankets will make your dog more comfortable during travels. You will also need water in the crate, as well as food, depending on how long the flight is. Your dog also needs identification on his collar at all times in case he gets lost.

Flying can be somewhat traumatic for a sensitive dog. If your dog is particularly sensitive to sounds, a loud cargo hold with changing temperatures may be hard on your canine friend. And, while dogs fly on a daily basis with few issues, there have been cases where dogs have been lost, left behind, or not taken to the correct pick-up point. Have the airline's contact information handy in case you need to locate your dog in an emergency. Also, it's a good idea to have a checkup before flying. If your dog is in ill health, he shouldn't fly. A veterinarian can give you the okay to travel, as well as prescribe any necessary medication that can make your dog's travels more comfortable.

Before departing, it's important to book a hotel where pets are welcomed. The last thing you want after a long trip is to be fined or kicked out of your accommodations for sneaking in a dog. Even worse would be to arrive at your hotel and learn your dog isn't welcome.

If you must leave your dog alone in the hotel room for any length of time, you will need to provide ample exercise for your pup. Otherwise, he may become bored and anxious, which is a recipe for disaster. In order to avoid paying fees for a destroyed room, take your dog for a long walk before you leave, and leave plenty of high-value chew toys in the room. If your dog is crate trained, this is a perfect use for a crate when you have to be away for a short period of time.

Kenneling vs. Dog Sitters

If you know that travel will be stressful for you and your dog, you may decide to leave your pup at home. It can be hard to leave a beloved pet at home when you're traveling, but it's often in your dog's best interest to do so. If you know you won't be able to spend a lot of time with your dog while you travel, your dog will be more comfortable spending time alone at home

Photo Courtesy of Breanna Fortner

CHAPTER 14   Traveling with Great Pyrenees

or at a kennel, as opposed to a strange hotel room. When leaving your dog at home, you have the option of boarding your pup at a kennel or hiring a dog sitter. The option you choose has a lot to do with your dog's personality.

If your dog is outgoing, friendly, and hates being alone, then a kennel may be your best option. These are facilities that provide your dog with a space to sleep and offer around-the-clock care. Someone will always have an eye on your dog, so you don't have to worry about your dog getting lonely. The best boarding facilities will give your dog lots of playtime and exercise, as well as allow your dog to play with other canines in their care. If your dog plays well with others, then he probably won't get too upset that he's not at home with you.

On the other hand, if your dog is sensitive to barking, gets nervous easily, and has a hard time making canine friends, a kennel can be overwhelmingly loud. If you're lucky to have dog-friendly friends and family members, consider asking them to look after your dog and make him feel at ease while you're away. If not, you can hire a dog sitter who can either come to your house to check in on your dog, or can board your dog in their house for more frequent attention.

When choosing a dog sitter, make sure they come to your home and meet your dog before you leave. That way, your Great Pyrenees won't mistake the sitter for an intruder. Choose a sitter who has good references and has plenty of time to spend with your dog. While an internet search can give you quick results for a sitter, you may also want to ask people in your community for recommendations. If a vet, trainer, or friend has good experience with someone, you may feel better about leaving your dog in the care of a stranger than if you choose someone off the internet.

Tips and Tricks for Traveling

Traveling with a dog has the potential to be stressful, but it doesn't have to be! If you're prepared, you'll find that a trip with your Great Pyrenees can be a lot of fun. When going on a long car trip with your dog, remember to tend to his needs. While you may be able to drive for a long stretch of time without breaks, your dog may get restless and will need to move around. A gas station may not have enough room for stretching legs and going to the bathroom, so plan at least one rest stop in a big, grassy area every four hours or so. Look for parks (and dog parks) along your route before you leave so you don't waste time looking while en route. During these breaks, make sure your dog has plenty of water.

Photo Courtesy of
Gilbert and Danielle Crawford
Double Dewclaw Ranch

Exercise is a valuable part of the travel experience. All of the new sights, sounds, and smells can really wind your dog up. Exercise helps calm nerves and keeps your dog's energy levels at a manageable level. Before you leave for your trip, take your dog on a long walk. That way, he'll be calm or sleepy as you travel. If you're taking a long drive, stop several times along the way to walk around. Once you get to your destination, take another walk to allow your dog to stretch his legs and get used to the new surroundings.

Make sure your dog's microchip information is up to date before you leave home. If your dog gets lost while you're away from home, you want to make sure the person who finds your dog has a way of identifying your dog and contacting you. Sometimes, a collar or tag can fall off, making it hard to find a dog's owner. If your dog doesn't have a microchip, a vet can do the procedure very quickly. If you've moved since chipping your dog, contact your vet or the microchip database company to update your phone number and address.

A checklist can help you stay organized when packing your dog's belongings for a trip. It's helpful to have a bag designated for your dog's belongings so you don't have to remember where you put everything. Here are a few things you don't want to leave home without.

- Food and water dishes
- Food and fresh water
- Treats
- Leash, collar, harness, car safety restraint, and identification tags
- Favorite toys and chews
- Crate and comfortable blanket
- Any medications or supplements as recommended by a vet

It can be a lot of fun to share your vacation with your Great Pyrenees, and proper preparation can ensure that the two of you have a safe and fun time. This dog isn't as portable as other smaller breeds, so you need to make sure your accommodations and transportation can support your giant dog. If you know that travel will be too much for your dog, or you know you won't be able to give your dog the attention he needs during your trip, find a boarder or sitter who can take excellent care of your dog while you're away.

CHAPTER 15
Nutrition

While it's simple to pour dog food into a dish a few times a day, it's important to give your dog the right foods in the correct amounts. Good nutrition can make all the difference in your dog's life and keep him out of the vet's office. Because dog nutrition is different than human nutrition, this chapter will give you the basic information you need to make choices about your dog's eating habits.

Importance of a Good Diet

This breed has very different nutritional needs, compared to a small-breed dog such as a Chihuahua. The Great Pyrenees is a high-energy creature, so your dog will need the right amount of calories. Too many, and he'll become overweight. Too few, and he'll be thin and lethargic.

Not all foods are created equal when it comes to the health of your dog. Some owners like to feed their dogs table scraps, which often provides an unpredictable mix of nutrients, and can include foods that can make a dog sick. For instance, too much fat and gristle can cause digestive distress. Also, not all manufactured dog foods have high-quality ingredients. Some have a wide variety of whole grains and different meats and fats, while others are mostly full of fillers.

Not all Great Pyrenees can eat the same foods. Food allergies are not extremely common in dogs, but some dogs cannot tolerate certain ingredients. If your dog appears ill after meals or has irregular bowel movements, the food may be to blame. If your dog has food allergies, you'll have to work with your vet and do some trial and error to find a dog food that works best for your pup.

What you put in your dog's dish matters. Unfortunately, feeding your dog isn't as simple as picking up whichever bag of dog food is on sale, or merely dumping your leftovers into your dog's dish. But, once you understand what your dog needs to be healthy, feeding your dog will be a breeze!

CHAPTER 15   Nutrition

Photo Courtesy of Marisa Alford

Good Foods for Great Pyrenees

"Dry food is best for dental their health. Puppies should receive a good large puppy breed Puppy Chow that is not excessively high in protein. Likewise the adults need a good quality large dog food, which is also not excessively high in protein. Their rapid growth combined with the high protein may contribute to some skeletal problems as they grow."

Susan Grimm
Grimm Acres, Diversified

Just like humans, dogs need carbohydrates, proteins, and fats, as well as vitamins and minerals. However, dogs need these nutrients in certain quantities. Breeder Susan Grimm of Grimm Acres recommends foods that don't have too much protein because protein contributes to rapid growth, which can lead to skeletal issues later on in life. Protein can come in different forms in dog foods. Chicken, beef, and fish are very common in commercial kibbles. Different meats have different nutrients, so a food with a good mix of meats can help ensure your dog is getting what he needs. For instance, red meats have plenty of iron, chicken is lean, and fish has healthy fats. Look for a dog food that has between twenty and thirty percent protein.

Carbohydrates give your dog energy. Quality dog foods tend to include a mix of simple and complex carbohydrates. Simple carbs, like the ones found in white rice, give your dog quick energy and are easy to digest. Complex carbs, like barley and oatmeal, contain fiber and keep your dog fuller and energized for longer. Some dogs have sensitivities to certain grains, so

CHAPTER 15   Nutrition

Photo Courtesy of Brittany McDowell & Steven Vail

some trial and error may take place before you find the right food. Grain-free formulas are popular because some dog owners believe that grains are harmful, but recent research suggests that these "grain-free formulas" can result in heart disease. Unless your veterinarian recommends feeding your dog one of these grain-free foods, stick to one that contains a healthy mix of carbohydrates.

Fats are also essential to your dog's overall wellbeing. When you read the ingredients lists, you might find it strange to see chicken fat on the list. However, fats are good sources of energy and make your dog's coat smooth and shiny. You may also see fats listed as fish oils or vegetable oils. These are all good sources of fats that contain different beneficial fatty acids.

It can be hard to know what your dog needs in his food, especially because the science of nutrition evolves on a frequent basis. With a large dog formula, you'll find a mix of vitamins and minerals to support your dog's big body. When in doubt, talk to your veterinarian. They will be able to tell you if your dog is missing anything in his diet, and point you in the direction of a good dog food or supplement as needed.

Different Types of Commercial Food

It can be overwhelming to walk down the dog food aisle at the pet store when the shelves are packed with a wide array of foods. With such a wide range of flavors, formulas, and prices, how is one to choose? Use the process of elimination to find a great formula for your pup.

First, consider your Great Pyrenees's life stage. If you have a puppy, he needs a special puppy formula for large breeds. Once your dog has reached

Photo Courtesy of Jessica Tyre

full size, switch over to an adult formula. Then, when your dog reaches old age, you may want to give your dog a senior formula to support his aging body's needs.

Next, make the choice between wet and dry food. Canned foods are very enticing to dogs because the moisture makes them especially fragrant. These wet foods are easy to eat, which makes them great for dogs with tooth problems, or other medical conditions that make eating hard. Plus, if you have a dog that is extremely stubborn and picky at mealtimes, wet food is often more appetizing.

However, it is not ideal to feed a dog a diet of only canned food. When a dog eats dry food, the scratchy texture scrapes plaque off teeth. When a dog eats wet food, there is no scraping action and the food sticks to the teeth. A combination of both foods is likely best, but talk to your vet.

Next, choose a brand. To narrow your selection down, you may want to talk to a vet or your breeder to see what they use for their dogs. If it's good enough for an expert's dogs, it's probably good enough for your pet.

Finally, choose a flavor. Some dogs are pickier than others. It can take a little time to figure out which flavors your dog likes best, and some formulas may work with your dog's digestive system better than others. If you choose a flavor that your dog isn't wild about, try another one. With so many options, it's hard for dogs not to get excited about a particular taste.

Homemade Foods

Some owners avoid commercial foods altogether and create their dog's meals from scratch. These meals tend to consist of meat, carbohydrates, and some fruits or vegetables, plus a vitamin and mineral supplement. This can be a healthy method of feeding, but the diet should be overseen by a veterinarian to ensure the dog is getting proper nutrition.

The benefit of a homemade diet is that you know exactly what's going into your dog's dish. You can choose the freshest ingredients from the healthiest sources and give your dog something you know he'll enjoy. If you don't want to worry about pet food recalls and suspicious ingredients, you may feel more at ease if you can control exactly what your dog eats.

One downside is that this method can be expensive and time consuming. Instead of buying a giant bag of kibble for the whole month, you'll have to make several trips to the store to get fresh meat. The ingredients in your daily meals are likely to be pricier than the couple of scoops of commercial dog food. And you'll need to be careful when feeding your dog, because commercial formulas are designed to have all of the nutrients a dog needs to be healthy. It's easy to omit a few nutrients when using whole food sources.

If you decide to go the homemade food route, it is imperative to discuss your recipe with your veterinarian so your dog doesn't miss out on any necessary nutrients.

People Foods—Harmful and Acceptable Kinds

Because so much thought goes into a dog's daily meals and training, you don't want to undo all of the healthy choices and hard work by feeding your dog table scraps. When you feed your dog from the table, you teach your dog that it's acceptable to eat human food, leading to bad behaviors. Also, you're adding calories and extra fat that your dog does not need.

If you decide to feed your dog scraps, at least do so in a way that does not teach your dog that he will be rewarded for begging. Save a few morsels in the fridge and use them for training treats later, or put them in his dish long after your own meal has ended. While dogs love eating fat trimmings and bones, both are detrimental to a dog's health. Bones can become choking hazards when they splinter, and too much fat is bad for your dog's internal organs. Chapter 3 has a list of common human foods that can make a dog seriously ill.

That doesn't mean that all people food is completely off limits. Some dogs go crazy for leafy greens, which are a great source of water, vitamins and minerals, and fiber. If your dog loves lettuce and spinach, you may decide to supplement their meal with a little garnish of greens. Or, if you're looking for healthy training treats, you might give your dog a blueberry or chunk of sweet potato every time he sits on command. These are low-calorie treats that pack a lot of essential nutrients.

Be mindful when giving your dog food that was not especially made for dogs. If you do it right, you can give your dog people foods in a way that improves your dog's health and reinforces good behaviors. Be careful, because it is very easy to reinforce naughty behaviors and give your dog foods that can make him ill, especially when he gives you his puppy eyes.

CHAPTER 15 Nutrition

Weight Management

All breeds have a healthy weight range where they can fluctuate between and still be healthy. However, if a dog gains too much weight, this puts undue stress on the skeletal system and internal organs. Over time, this can put a lot of strain on the body.

Your veterinarian can tell you if your dog is a healthy weight at regular checkups, but you can also keep an eye on your dog in between visits. You never want your dog to be so thin that you can see his ribs, but you do want to be able to feel them when you apply gentle pressure. When you look at your dog from above, his body should tuck in at the waist. If your dog is too round, he is probably overweight. All of the fluff on your Great Pyrenees can make it hard to distinguish his body type, so give your dog a quick examination when his fur is wet from a bath.

> **FUN FACT**
> **Brewmaster's Dog**
>
> Sea Dog Brewing Company, headquartered in Maine, sports a Great Pyrenees dog in a yellow sou'wester hat as their logo. This logo represents Barney, the mascot of the company and pet of the company's founder, Pete Camplin Sr. It's said that Barney served as an apprentice to the brewmaster and stood watch over the brew kettle.

If your dog is overweight, you'll need to reduce calories and increase exercise. However, if your dog goes from sedentary to going on jogs, he's likely to get overheated. Increase your exercise a little every day until your dog gets into better shape. Also, consider all of your dog's calorie sources. Do you overfeed your dog during meals or does he eat too many high-calorie treats or table scraps? Try to limit extras. If you change your dog's habits and he's still chunky, your dog may need a special weight-control dog food, or there could be a medical issue. Your vet will be able to confirm a weight problem and help you get your dog back into a healthy size.

There's a lot to think about when it comes to feeding your dog, but it doesn't have to be complicated. The easiest way to find a good dog food is to ask a vet or breeder for a recommendation. Some dogs have sensitivities that make special formulas necessary, but this is not the norm. Most dogs will do just fine with a dry, middle-range dog food formula. Of course, if you have any concerns about your dog's nutrition, consult with a vet.

CHAPTER 16
Grooming Your Great Pyrenees

"Pyrenees have a double coat. The inner code is thick fine and Wooly while the outer coat is longer hair similar to other dogs. When the seasons change and when the dogs occasionally blow their coat, the undercoat can come out in huge a mass which needs to be combed or raked out from under their outer coat. For dogs that will be in the house, a regular grooming schedule is essential as well as a quality vacuum cleaner."

Susan Grimm
Grimm Acres, Diversified

CHAPTER 16 Grooming Your Great Pyrenees

Grooming isn't only beneficial for your dog's good looks—it's also great for his health and comfort. Clean ears and teeth reduce the chance of infection that can lead to serious health issues, and brushed fur can keep your dog from painful knots and mats. Plus, brushing and bathing your dog will reduce the amount of dirt, fur, and odors that cover your home and all of your belongings! This breed requires more grooming than others, because of the Great Pyrenees's long, fluffy coat, but grooming doesn't have to be a chore. If you keep up with your dog's grooming on a regular basis, you won't have to worry about cutting out mats or frequent professional teeth cleanings. This chapter will teach you how to keep your dog looking and feeling fresh.

Coat Basics

The Great Pyrenees has a thick double coat. This means that underneath the sleek top coat is a fine and thick layer of insulation. This fur is so soft and readily available that some people even collect the fur to spin into yarn! The undercoat is very important for this breed as it keeps the dog both warm in the winter and cool in the summer. While brushing is necessary to remove shedding fur, it is unnecessary to shave this dog. Some well-meaning dog owners shed their fluffy dogs to keep them cool in hot weather, but this only leaves them more vulnerable to the elements. If your dog appears to be too hot, it's best to give him shade, cool water, and air conditioning.

Your Great Pyrenees's coat is magical. According to breeder Lindsey Morrison of Golden Pond Farms, this breed's coat is self-maintaining. Dirt, water, and odors seem to fly right off this dog. This will make it easier for you to keep your dog's coat clean. The occasional bath may still be necessary, but most of the time, you can keep your pup clean with a quick brushing and perhaps a quick wipe with a damp towel.

A few times a year, your Great Pyrenees will blow his coat. This means that he will shed a lot of fur in a short amount of time. You may want to add a good vacuum cleaner and lint roller to your list of pet supplies, because the breed will certainly leave a lot of fluff behind! Regular brushing can reduce some of this mess. Take your dog to the backyard and give him a good brushing. He'll enjoy how the brush feels on his skin and you'll prevent clumps of fur from finding their way to your carpet.

You'll want a few different brushes in your arsenal. A rake is useful for quick de-fluffing. This gets right down to the undercoat to remove dead fur before it has the chance to clump up and cause matting. This tool has a few

rows of tightly spaced pins that quickly take out extra fur. You will also want to have a slicker brush to prevent or remove mats. This brush has long, thin bristles that work through tangles. You may also want a pin brush, which is like a human's hairbrush, to smooth your dog's coat and remove loose topcoat. However, this type of brush won't get deep enough to the skin to remove a lot of undercoat. Brush your dog's fur several times a week to keep his coat shiny and keep tangles under control.

Bathing

In general, dogs do not need frequent baths. Of course, exceptions can be made if your dog rolls around in a mud puddle or in something stinky, but otherwise, four baths a year should be sufficient. Save the water for when your dog really needs it; otherwise, you'll be stripping natural oils from your dog's coat.

When choosing a shampoo, it's best to buy one that's simple and gentle. Buy shampoo specifically made for dogs, as human hair products may be too harsh on your dog's skin. If your dog's white coat is important to you, there are dog shampoos that are made to brighten and whiten a dingy coat. There are tons of shampoos out there with different scents and purposes, but some ingredients can irritate a dog's skin, especially if he has allergies. Don't worry about buying the high-end, fancy shampoos and conditioners

CHAPTER 16   Grooming Your Great Pyrenees

either—your dog will only get a handful of baths per year, and your aim is to get any extra dirt and odor off his fur.

Some dogs do not like baths, so anything you can do to make the bath an easy and positive experience is necessary. A shower head with a detachable hose will make baths much easier, as opposed to continuously filling and dumping cups of water on your dog. Also, remember to use treats to keep your dog happy. If your pup is especially fidgety, a small smearing of peanut butter on the wall of your shower will keep him still and occupied for a while. When the bath is over, give your dog another treat or reward him with playtime. That way, he doesn't associate baths with unpleasant sensations.

When bathing your dog, make sure to thoroughly rinse the shampoo out of your dog's fur. Shampoo residue will make your dog's coat dull and make his skin dry and itchy. Rinse until you no longer see suds, then rinse a little more, just to be certain the soap is gone. Also, be careful not to get water in his ears and eyes. Instead of rinsing your dog's head and face, use a damp cloth to gently clean around those sensitive areas.

Photo Courtesy of Jillian Olsen

Trimming Nails

Whether you take your dog to a groomer to have his nails trimmed or you take on the task at home, your pup will need to have his toenails clipped on a regular basis. Not only will long nails leave scratches on everything, but they can cause damage to your dog's paws. When your dog walks around on long nails, it places a lot of stress on the foot, and can cause pain and inflammation later on. So it's important to keep your dog's nails trimmed so that they do not touch the ground.

This is a fairly simple task, but it makes many dog owners nervous because of the potential to cut the nails too short and cause pain and bleeding. With the nail clippers, carefully clip small pieces of the toenail until it no longer touches the ground when your dog is standing. Cut too far, and you'll nick the quick, or blood supply to the nail. The pink quick is visible in dogs with white or clear nails, but harder to locate in dogs with black nails.

Many dogs are hesitant to have their nails cut, which results in a lot of squirming. To make cutting nails easier, train your dog to relax and sit still

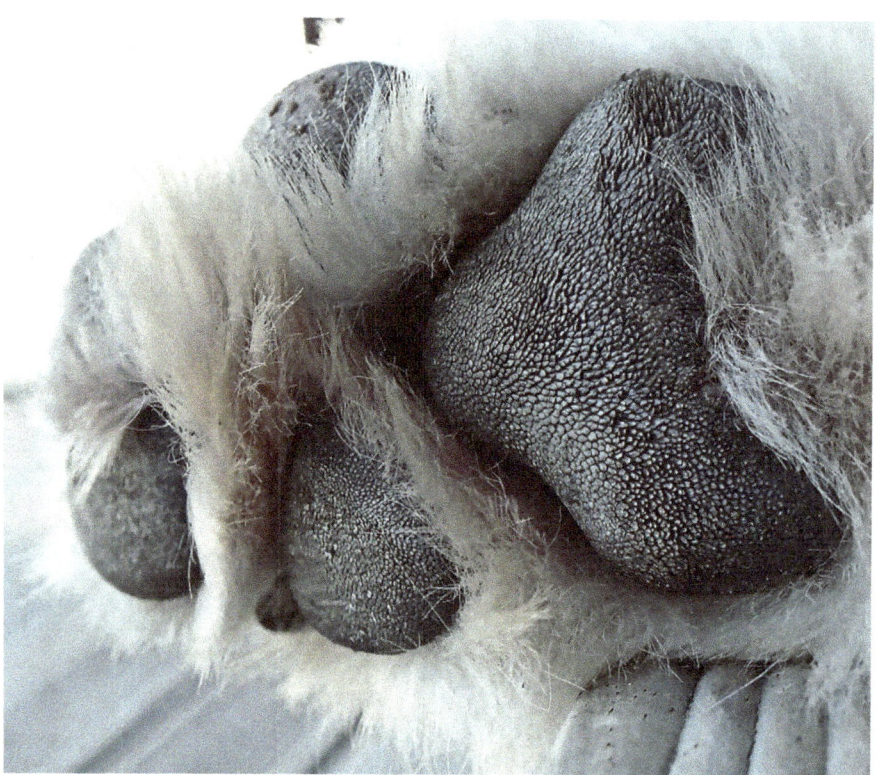

during the chore. Before you even make a cut, place the clippers near your dog and give him a treat if he is calm or doesn't seem to mind the tool in his vicinity. Work your way up to holding his paw or merely touching the clippers to his nails. Once he is used to the clippers, trim a nail and give him lots of praise and treats for sitting still. If he can't sit still while you cut all of his nails, do a paw or two at a time and give him a break before finishing the job—you don't want your dog to associate nail clipping with negative feelings. Great Pyrenees have an extra dew claw that also needs to be clipped. While it won't ever touch the ground, it can curl around and cause problems if left to grow.

If you're nervous about cutting your dog's nails, take him to a groomer. An experienced groomer will be able to do the job efficiently without cutting the nails too short or upsetting your dog. If your dog is so squirmy that you struggle to get the job done, or you're petrified of drawing blood, the best thing to do is find a trusted groomer to help you.

Brushing Teeth

Clean teeth are not only important for your puppy's pretty smile. A buildup of plaque and bacteria can lead to tooth decay, which can be very painful and affect how your dog eats. Heart disease can also be aggravated by poor dental hygiene.

Dog toothbrushes have angled handles and small brush heads, making it easy to reach all of the teeth. You may find that a child's toothbrush also works well. There are even rubber-bristled brushes that you can slip over your finger if a more hands-on approach is easier for you.

> **HELPFUL TIP**
> **Dental Wipes**
>
> Dogs, like humans, see many benefits from having good dental hygiene. Since dogs aren't able to care for their own teeth, it falls on responsible pet owners to develop a strategy for their dogs' dental care routine. One option for keeping your dog's teeth and gums healthy is dental wipes. These disposable wipes provide a convenient alternative to a toothbrush and toothpaste for dogs who are not accustomed to having their teeth brushed, or who require a gentler form of cleaning. Talk with your vet about the right choice for you and your dog.

Then, you'll need a good toothpaste. Human toothpaste is not good for dogs because it contains toxic chemicals that a dog can't spit out when they foam. Dog toothpastes are formulated with enzymes that are safe to swallow. They also come in dog-friendly flavors like peanut butter or chicken.

When you brush your dog's teeth, focus on the outer, visible parts of the tooth. Your dog's crunchy food should do a good job scraping plaque off the other surfaces. Brush gently for a few minutes, several times a week. If you can establish daily brushing into your routine, that's great! However, if you aim for just two to three times a week, your dog should still have clean teeth, fresh breath, and require fewer professional cleanings.

Cleaning Ears and Eyes

There isn't a lot for an owner to do to keep a dog's ears and eyes healthy, but it's a good idea to know the signs of irritation or infection so you know when to take your dog to the vet. Some dogs, especially those with white fur, may get tear stains underneath their eyes. To clean up gunk, carefully wipe under the eyes with a damp cloth, taking care not to get too close to the eye. If your dog's eyes are especially watery or have unusual discharge, this may be a sign of infection and should be assessed by a vet. Otherwise, your dog's eyes should need no attention from you.

Ears are a slightly different story. Any dog with floppy ears has an increased risk of ear infections. This tends to occur when moisture becomes trapped inside of the ear. The moist, warm environment becomes a breeding ground for bacteria that can cause itchiness and pain. If you notice that your dog has wet ears, like after a swim, carefully dry the flap of the ear with a gentle cloth or cotton ball. Never use a cotton swab or other small object to clean deeper into your dog's ear.

If you see a buildup of wax or mild redness, your vet may recommend that you wash your dog's ears between checkups. Pet stores sell ear cleaning solutions for home use. Simply squirt the solution directly into your dog's ear and give it a good massage. This will break up all of the wax in the ear. Then, allow your dog to shake his head in order to remove the wax. Finish up by wiping any extra waxy residue from the outer part of the ear. There's a good chance your dog will not like the sensation of having a cold liquid squirted into his ear, so give him a treat afterward so he will sit still for you the next time. If redness and irritation persist, it's never a bad idea to have your vet take a look at your dog's ears to tell you if your dog needs further treatment.

When Professional Help Is Necessary

If your dog is particularly hard to manage during grooming time, you may want to have him bathed and get his nails clipped at a groomer. For instance, if you're not comfortable trimming your dog's nails because you're afraid you're going to cut too far, it's worth it to spend a little extra money to have a professional take care of it. Or, if it's a struggle to put your giant dog in your little shower for a bath, you may decide it's easier to take your dog to the groomer a few times a year for a good scrubbing. Grooming at home saves money, but it's only worth it if you actually do the work. If you can't accomplish some of the tasks in your home (or just prefer not to) you can outsource this work to a professional.

Grooming is an extremely important part of dog ownership. If you dedicate a half hour or so per week to the task, you shouldn't have many problems with your dog's coat or overall hygiene. Not only does grooming keep you dog looking nice, but it will also help him feel comfortable and stay healthy. If you find that grooming is too much for you to take on by yourself, remember that there are lots of experienced professionals who would be happy to help you keep your Great Pyrenees looking fresh.

CHAPTER 17
Basic Health Care

There are few things more important than your dog's health. When it comes to taking care of your dog's body, prevention is best. Taking your dog for regular checkups, keeping up to date on shots and preventative medications, and staying on top of your dog's hygiene will save you time, money, and worry. It's important to have a basic knowledge of health concerns in Great Pyrenees so you know what to look out for. Also, it's important to have a good relationship with a veterinarian or clinic so you feel certain that your vet will catch any concerns you miss. This chapter will cover some important things you need to know about your Great Pyrenees's health.

Photo Courtesy of Jan Betz

CHAPTER 17   Basic Health Care

Visiting the Vet

Your vet is a fantastic resource for all things regarding your Great Pyrenees. However, there are some reasons why dog owners don't bring their pooch to the vet as often as they should. For starters, many dogs get nervous at the vet. To ease your dog's nervousness, first make sure that he is comfortable riding in a car before you go. Once you've cleared that hurdle, continue to give your dog treats and praise when you enter the clinic. Your vet will likely also give your dog treats, too. Once the checkup is over, give your dog lots of play time. You may also want to give your dog play time before the vet to burn any extra energy that can result in nervous behavior.

Other owners avoid regular checkups because they can be expensive. Fortunately, veterinary billing is much simpler than the human doctor's office. Before you even step foot in the office, you should be able to ask about the price of whatever procedures are taking place. If your vet recommends any procedures, tests, or medications, you can ask for the price before agreeing to the service. This should ease owner anxiety about not knowing how much a trip to the vet will cost. If the cost is an issue for you, talk to your vet about the different payment plans they offer.

When you take your dog in for a checkup, your vet will do a quick look over your dog while asking you questions about any concerns you may have. During this check, the vet will look at your dog's eyes, ears, and mouth, while also feeling your dog's belly. Your vet will also listen to your dog's heart and breathing with a stethoscope, and take your dog's temperature. These things may feel intrusive to your dog, so you may want to practice before going to the vet so your dog knows what's coming. Practice flipping your dog's ears back and lifting his lips to see his teeth. Run your hands along your dog's body and gently palpate his belly. Have him stand still while you put one hand on his chest. This may keep your dog from being alarmed when a stranger touches him because he's already experienced it with you.

Your vet will have a record of your dog's vaccinations, so he'll be able to tell you if your dog needs any shots. Your vet will also give your dog a yearly blood test to check for heartworm. Once your vet gets a good look at your dog, he'll be able to recommend any further services or prescriptions. Use this time to discuss all of your concerns about your dog, even the minor ones. You never know which symptoms can amount to greater problems.

Fleas and Ticks

Because Great Pyrenees love to spend time outside, it is possible that your pup will come across fleas or ticks at some point in his life. These bugs are particularly bad because they can cause illness or skin reactions. Luckily, you can give your dog a preventative medication that repels or kills these pests before they can cause more problems.

Depending on which method your vet recommends, you can buy an oral medication or a topical treatment to put on your dog's skin once a month. It is important to give your dog the preventative every month so your dog remains protected. The cost of the preventative adds up over time, but the price is worth it if you don't have to pick fleas out of your dog's thick coat.

If the preventative doesn't work and your dog ends up with ticks or fleas, it's important to take care of it right away. Ticks aren't terribly hard to remove; simply grasp toward the head, near your dog's skin, and give a firm, yet slow pull. Once you've removed the insect, crush it with a rock or other hard object to kill it. Ticks are hard to kill, so make sure they're dead before disposing of them. Fleas are a much bigger challenge. These insects proliferate like crazy and are good at hiding. Once your dog has been given medication, you'll have to comb through your dog's fur with a flea comb to remove any of the fleas. Then you'll need to give your dog a good scrub with flea shampoo to kill any leftover fleas or eggs. Finally, you'll need to

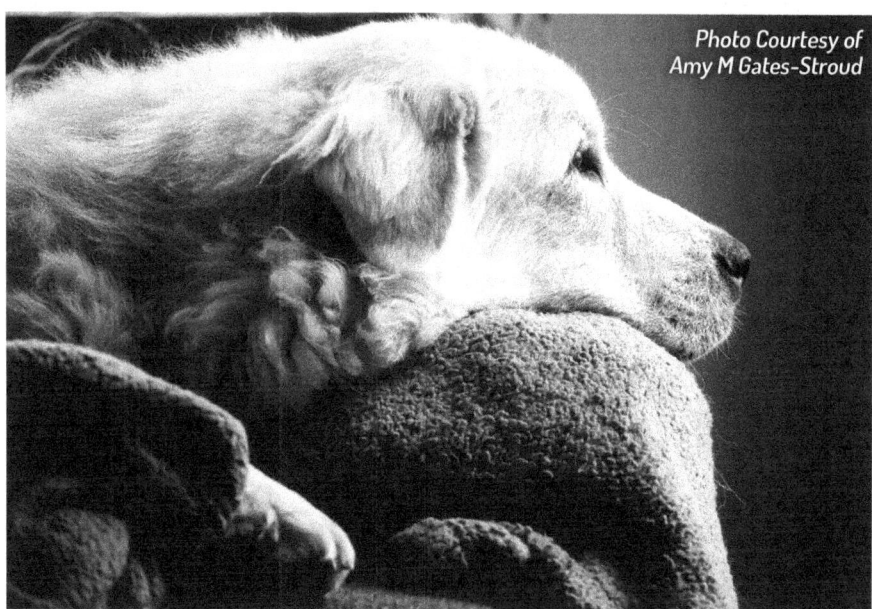

Photo Courtesy of Amy M Gates-Stroud

do a thorough cleaning that lasts several days after you last see fleas, as eggs can hide in furniture or floorboards and reemerge. Wash everything in hot water, vacuum daily, and use cleaning products meant for flea removal. This eradication process can last weeks, so remember that when you're debating whether or not to buy flea and tick preventative!

Worms and Parasites

In addition to external parasites, dogs can also acquire parasitic creatures that feed on your dog from the inside. Intestinal worms are fairly common in puppies, so many puppies from breeders or shelters will probably have a deworming treatment before they find their way into your home. If you notice worms in your dog's stool, you need to take your dog to the vet to get medication. Your vet will likely want you to collect a stool sample so he can see what exactly is feeding on your dog's insides. Lethargy, change in stools, and a lack of appetite are all symptoms of intestinal worms. Luckily, this is treatable and your dog will be feeling more like himself once he gets medication.

> **HELPFUL TIP**
> **Signs of Bloat**
>
> Bloat is an uncomfortable and sometimes deadly condition in dogs that requires prompt treatment. Symptoms of bloat include pacing, anxiety, drooling, restlessness, swollen stomach, and unproductive heaving. If you notice these symptoms, or your dog becomes weak or collapses, seek immediate medical attention for your dog.

Heartworm is a serious concern in dogs because it can be fatal if left untreated. These are worms that are introduced through the bloodstream, typically through a mosquito bite. The worms make their way to the heart, where they cause damage. Cough, fatigue, lack of appetite, and weight loss are all symptoms of heartworm. Heartworm is a treatable condition, but it must be caught before the worms cause heart failure. Fortunately, this disease is preventable. With one tablet a month, your dog will be safe from acquiring heartworm. Your vet will want to do a blood test on a yearly basis before prescribing more heartworm preventative, so you can be sure your dog is in the clear on an annual basis. It is important to give this pill every month on the same day, so be sure to write a note on your calendar so you remember to give your dog his medication. The cost of these pills also adds up, but it's still cheaper than dealing with heartworm and all of the negative effects it has on your dog.

Common Diseases Found in Great Pyrenees

"Hip or elbow dysplasia can be common in some. We always test our breeding adults at 2 years of age for their hips and elbows. That does not guarantee that their puppies will never be affected, but it does help."

Lindsey Morrison
Golden Pond Farms

While a Great Pyrenees puppy from a trustworthy breeder should be clear of health concerns, there are a few diseases that are prominent in this breed.

Perhaps the most common disease found in big dogs is hip dysplasia. This condition occurs when the hip socket and leg bone do not fit together correctly. This can cause a lot of pain and a loss of range of motion. As your dog gets older, the joint will become increasingly painful from overuse. Your breeder will be able to tell you if she tests her dogs for hip dysplasia. Apart from genetics, this condition may be aggravated by growing too quickly, a side effect of improper nutrition. If your dog has a hard time getting around as he ages, talk to your vet about what you can do to reduce your dog's discomfort.

Lindsey Morrison of Golden Pond Farms cites bone cancer as a concern in Great Pyrenees. Symptoms are likely to appear as your dog becomes older, around eight to eleven. A dog with bone cancer may begin to limp, depending on where the cancer has formed in his body. You may also see swelling where the cancer has metastasized. If the cancer is in a limb, amputation may be encouraged to reduce the intense pain. Chemotherapy and radiation therapies may also be administered. This cancer spreads quickly, so the quicker it is treated, the better the outcome.

Morrison has also noticed eye entropion in some puppies. This is a condition that occurs when part of the eyelid is folded inward. This is not a life-threatening condition, but it does cause eyelashes or hair to scratch the surface of the eye, which can be uncomfortable and cause infections. This can be fixed with surgery.

Susie Wong of Darlington Great Pyrenees lists neuronal degeneration as a condition to watch out for in Great Pyrenees. This is a genetic neurological disease that shows symptoms from a young age. Dogs with this disease will have a hard time moving around smooth surfaces, have an abnormal gait, and seem generally weak and uncoordinated. As it progresses, the dog will have a lack of coordination and may fall. Not a lot is known about this condition, but it's something to look out for if you feel as though your dog is not getting around as well as usual.

There are many ailments that dogs can suffer from, but some are more common in certain breeds than others. It's completely possible that your Great Pyrenees will live a long and happy life without any of these conditions. It's good to know what to watch out for, though, just in case your dog displays symptoms of an illness. When in doubt, call the vet or bring your dog in for an appointment. When it comes to your dog's good health, it's better to be safe than sorry.

Vaccinations

Vaccinations are a necessary part of dog ownership. Without vaccinations, your dog is left vulnerable to contract all sorts of nasty illnesses. Vaccinations are a small price to pay for the peace of mind you'll have when you know your dog will not contract kennel cough after a trip to the dog park. Another benefit of vaccines is that they keep your dog from spreading illness to other dogs. Herd immunity can protect dogs that have not been vaccinated, like young puppies.

The rabies vaccine is one that is not negotiable. In order to license your dog, you must have your dog up to date on his rabies booster. You will also need this life-saving vaccination to be able to participate in training classes and enter some dog parks. If you have any hesitations about vaccinating your pup, talk to your vet. You'll find that these miracles of modern medicine will keep your dog happy and healthy for many years to come.

Basics of Senior Dog Care

Because giant breeds like the Great Pyrenees have shorter lives than small breeds, they may be considered senior around the age of six or seven. This doesn't mean that your dog can no longer have fun and be playful, but you will need to take some precautions into account as your dog ages.

For starters, your dog's nutritional needs may change. Your vet may even suggest a senior dog food formula. Senior dogs tend to be less active, so they need fewer calories. If your old dog starts packing on the pounds, you may need to reduce the amount of food he gets.

Photo Courtesy of Nikki Proctor

Exercise needs may also change. Young pups can run for hours, but older dogs move a little slower and get tired easier. Even though you're able to walk at your same pace and distance, you'll need to remember to slow down for your old dog. Your dog may think he can chase a ball like a puppy, but he may feel stiff and sore the next day. If your dog is slowing down, be sure to take it easy.

When dogs age, they can sometimes show mental signs of aging, just like in humans. Keep your dog's brain sharp by playing puzzle games with high-value treats inside. A Kong toy with peanut butter can also keep your dog entertained without requiring a lot of work. Your dog may take more naps than he did as a young adult, but he can still get bored if he doesn't get the mental stimulation he needs.

In general, you will want to be more careful with your old dog, especially if he has issues with joint pain. Long toenails can put a lot of pressure on paws, so it's especially important to keep nails trimmed. When your dog rests on the floor, his thin blanket won't feel as comfortable as it used to. You may need to get a thicker bed to cushion your dog's body. If your dog once jumped from the bed to the floor, make sure he doesn't injure himself as his joints wear out and consider pet stairs.

More than anything, your dog still wants the love and attention he got during earlier life stages. Your dog may be aging, but that doesn't mean that you can no longer have adventures together. Continue with your normal routine, but pay attention to signs that your dog needs modifications in his daily activities.

When It's Time to Say Goodbye

If your dog does not pass from natural causes, you may have to make a difficult decision at a certain time. No owner wants to make this call, but it can sometimes be necessary if your dog is suffering.

One sign that it's time to say goodbye is if your dog can no longer move around on his own. If your dog's limbs hurt so much that he cannot get up and

CHAPTER 17 Basic Health Care

walk on his own, it may be time to take your dog to be put down. Oftentimes, dogs minimize their pain, so if they are visibly in pain, you know that it's serious. Another sign that the end is near is when your dog can no longer to go the bathroom outside. If your dog is having a few accidents, it's not that big of a deal. But if your dog has serious incontinence, you may have to make a decision. In the end, you have to make a decision based on your dog's quality of life.

Of course, this is a discussion you want to have with your vet. Sometimes the ailments you assume are signs of end-of-life can be treated. But if there is nothing you or your vet can do to make your old dog comfortable, it may be time to say goodbye. The euthanasia process is quick and painless for a dog. The vet will inject the dog with a drug that will quickly cause the dog to lose consciousness. Within minutes, heart and brain functions cease. It is not required for an owner to be in the room when euthanasia occurs, but it may be comforting for the dog to have a familiar friend by his side. This is an extremely difficult time for an owner, but know that this end-of-life care may come as a great relief for a suffering animal.

Having a Great Pyrenees for a best friend can be a very rewarding experience. These gorgeous, energetic dogs are a lot of fun and can make a great addition to your family. These dogs love to work and will go to great lengths to protect his people. Owning one of these dogs can be a ton of work and requires a lot of patience. However, the work you put into training, grooming, and healthcare will be well worth it. Your new dog has a lot of love to give, and you'll be sure to enjoy every moment of life with your new best friend.

Photo Courtesy of Beth Jensen